A Retrospective View and Consideration of India Affairs

Particularly of the Transactions of the Mharatta War, from its Commencement to the Month of October, 1782

Anonymous

CAMBRIDGE UNIVERSITY PRESS

Cambridge, New York, Melbourne, Madrid, Cape Town, Singapore,
São Paolo, Delhi, Dubai, Tokyo, Mexico City

Published in the United States of America by Cambridge University Press, New York

www.cambridge.org
Information on this title: www.cambridge.org/9781108027106

© in this compilation Cambridge University Press 2010

This edition first published 1783
This digitally printed version 2010

ISBN 978-1-108-02710-6 Paperback

This book reproduces the text of the original edition. The content and language reflect
the beliefs, practices and terminology of their time, and have not been updated.

Cambridge University Press wishes to make clear that the book, unless originally published
by Cambridge, is not being republished by, in association or collaboration with, or
with the endorsement or approval of, the original publisher or its successors in title.

CAMBRIDGE LIBRARY COLLECTION

Books of enduring scholarly value

History

The books reissued in this series include accounts of historical events and movements by eye-witnesses and contemporaries, as well as landmark studies that assembled significant source materials or developed new historiographical methods. The series includes work in social, political and military history on a wide range of periods and regions, giving modern scholars ready access to influential publications of the past.

A Retrospective View and Consideration of India Affairs

This anonymous work was published at the end of the First Anglo-Maratha war (1775–82) to provide an English audience with a better understanding of the recent conflict. The author (who may have been a Major John Scott, and is likely to have been connected to the East India Company) is at times quite critical of the Company and some of the decisions which were made in relation to the conduct of the war. He suggests that India-based employees were not always giving the whole picture to the directors in England. He argues that war could have been avoided (blaming Warren Hastings, the governor-general of Bengal, for its outbreak), and that Britain had done badly out of negotiations for peace. The book is an early source of information about the Indian states which were soon to become incorporated into British India, and on Anglo-Indian relations.

Cambridge University Press has long been a pioneer in the reissuing of out-of-print titles from its own backlist, producing digital reprints of books that are still sought after by scholars and students but could not be reprinted economically using traditional technology. The Cambridge Library Collection extends this activity to a wider range of books which are still of importance to researchers and professionals, either for the source material they contain, or as landmarks in the history of their academic discipline.

Drawing from the world-renowned collections in the Cambridge University Library, and guided by the advice of experts in each subject area, Cambridge University Press is using state-of-the-art scanning machines in its own Printing House to capture the content of each book selected for inclusion. The files are processed to give a consistently clear, crisp image, and the books finished to the high quality standard for which the Press is recognised around the world. The latest print-on-demand technology ensures that the books will remain available indefinitely, and that orders for single or multiple copies can quickly be supplied.

The Cambridge Library Collection will bring back to life books of enduring scholarly value (including out-of-copyright works originally issued by other publishers) across a wide range of disciplines in the humanities and social sciences and in science and technology.

A

RETROSPECTIVE VIEW

AND

CONSIDERATION

OF

INDIA AFFAIRS;

PARTICULARLY OF THE

TRANSACTIONS

OF THE

MHARATTA WAR,

FROM ITS

COMMENCEMENT

TO THE

MONTH OF OCTOBER, 1782.

LONDON:

PRINTED FOR J. DEBRETT, OPPOSITE BURLINGTON-HOUSE,
PICCADILLY, AND J. SEWELL, CORNHILL.

MDCCLXXXIII.

PREFACE.

THE writer of the following sheets, in submitting them to the confideration of the public, feels himfelf more influenced by zeal for the community, than by any views of a private or perfonal nature. He is therefore little folicitous of literary rewards, or interefted in the reputation he is likely to obtain as an author, farther than as fuch a wifh may be connected with that ftrict regard to truth and juftice, which is the chief object of his ambition, and the only qualification effentially equifite to conftitute the character to which he afpires.

If the impartial relation of circumftances to which h has adhered fhould fortunately refcue one fact from the mift of falfhood, with which the arts of defigning and interefted men have laboured to difguife it, or affift in doing juftice to the conduct of one individual, who might otherwife fall a victim to the fecret fhafts of envy, and the malicious rancour of party, he will enjoy a confcious and heart-felt pleafure, fuperior to every other poffible gratification, and confider fuch a recompenfe as fully proportioned to the affiduity and anxious trouble with which he has collected, compared and arranged the several materials of which the present narrative is composed.

His satisfaction will be perfect, and his reward complete, if by an early and candid exposition of the state of affairs in India, and of the several political transactions which have led thereto, he should be so happy as to furnish any information of the smallest public utility, and tending to point out the means of either remedying past evils, or preventing a repetion of similar disasters hereafter.

It is with this animating hope that he presumes to address the Honourable Court of Directors of the United East-India Company upon the present occasion, and to submit the following production to their particular attention and consideration, convinced that the watchful care and ardent zeal, with which they are accustomed to superintend and promote the important interests committed to their management and direction, will make them gladly and favourably listen to whatever bears an appearance of contributing to advance the same desirable object, and that at all events, their well-known candour and generosity of sentiment, will make every indulgent and liberal allowance, and pardon any defect in the performance itself, in consideration of the motives from which it originated.

A

RETROSPECTIVE VIEW

AND

CONSIDERATION

OF

INDIA AFFAIRS.

A FAITHFUL account of the Mharatta war, including every material tranfaction of a military as well as political nature, that has occurred in India for above eight years paft, muft at this juncture prove a pleafing and interefting fubject, and be of infinite ufe to throw a juft light upon thofe important points, which are at prefent the objects of public enquiry and difcuffion, and in obtaining a certain knowledge of which, national juftice, no lefs than that due to many individuals of character and ftation in the Company's fervice, is fo effentially concerned.

The magnitude and difficulty of the tafk, though it excites my apprehenfion, cannot deter me from the attempt; becaufe, however defective my narrative may be found in the exterior ornaments of ftyle and grace of compofition, it will (I am confcious) be dictated by the warmeft and moft zealous wifhes for the intereſts of my country, by a mind totally divested of all prejudice or partiality whatever, and by an actual knowledge of most of the important facts that are related, which is derived either from personal observation, or from such authentic papers and vouchers, as are positive and incontrovertible.

To the encouragement this consideration gives me, is added another motive still more animating, when I reflect that this narrative is expressly intended for the perusal of the Company's representatives at home, and upon a subject which they have deemed deserving of the most particular and careful attention, and will, on that account, no less than from their acknowledged candor and liberality, receive, with flattering satisfaction, every information regarding it, that bears evident marks of truth and moderation of temper.

I shall not take up more time in the dull formality of a preface, but after explaining in few words the nature and extent of the present work, enter immediately into a detail of circumstances, avoiding as much as possible any impertinent or unnecessary intrusion upon the patience of the public, as well as every attempt to bias or influence their judgments, either by offering opinions which are obvious and self evident, or by putting such interpretation and gloss upon facts, as might disguise their true colour, and best serve any particular and partial purpose.

It is to a clear and exact, though not circumstantial, relation of facts I mean to confine myself. I shall endeavour to shew the consequences of every military and political effort, and the advantages and disappointments respectively produced by them, without minutely describing the operations of the campaign, or the intrigues of the cabinet, farther than may be necessary

to

to point out the errors of the particular fyftems from which the latter may have originated, and to prove the misfortunes that have ultimately flowed from them.

A more extenfive plan might encreafe and embellifh the fubject, but would not anfwer any ufeful purpofe of information, which is the fole end I have in view, and with the hope of which alone I am animated to enter upon the prefent tafk with zeal and chearfulnefs.

The frequent occafion I fhall have in the courfe of this narrative to mention the Mharattas, their great power as a nation, and indeed the circumftance of its being entirely owing to the fyftem originally adopted by the Company's fervants in India regarding them, that their affairs are at prefent fo critically and alarmingly fituated, renders fome account of their government in this place highly proper and requifite.

The origin and foundation of their empire is a fubject rather of curiofity and amufing fpeculation than of ufeful enquiry; it cannot therefore properly belong to this place: and were I even difpofed to difplay my talents for hiftorical inveftigation, and the induftry with which I have exerted them, I fhould on this occafion decline fuch an attempt, and acknowledge it anticipated by a production which I have lately feen, publifhed by an officer of the Bombay eftablifhment, and containing the moft reafonable, and (I believe) genuine account of the original formation and fubfequent rife of the Mharatta power, which has yet been obtained by the European enquirer. I fhall therefore only touch upon the fubject, and in the moft general terms.

The mode of government eftablifhed by its firft great founder, Sahou or Sewajie, proved to be of no long duration; for although the name of fovereignty ftill remains with the Rajah, and each fucceeding Peifhwa receives the inveftiture of that office from his hands, according to the ceremonious forms originally practifed; this mark of fuperiority and attention is almoft the only one at prefent obferved; and the real power of the ftate, together with the entire control and management of affairs, is exercifed and conducted by, and under the exprefs authority of, the Peifhwa, who keeps his court at Poonah. This place is at prefent confidered as the capital of the Mharatta empire, fince the Rajah, who conftantly refides at Settara, a ftrong and almoft inacceffible fortrefs about fixty miles diftant, is never permitted to ftir out of the latter, but like the bird in its gilded cage, is dazzled and amufed by the falfe glare of external ceremony and refpect, which only ferves to make the gloom and wretchednefs of his prifon more confpicuoufly fplendid.

There is perhaps fcarce any family in the hiftory of mankind, which has produced an equal number of illuftrious and able characters to that of the prefent reigning Peifhwa. It was to the addrefs and influence of its founder, Ballajee Pundit, that Rajah Sahou was indebted for the eftablifhment as well as growth of his empire, and gratitude at firft made him repofe a confidence in his benefactor, which habits of indolence towards the latter part of his life, and the ability and talents of the other, improved into a total relaxation from the care and fatigue of bufinefs on his own part, and a delegation of his authority to the Peifhwa. The fucceffors of the latter treading in his footfteps, have transferred this authority to themfelves as matter of right, and a precedent to eftablifh the fovereign power at prefent exercifed by them.

An adminiftration formed and conducted by men of the character above mentioned, and which, to other engines of a defpotic and uncontrolable will, unites that of religion, the moft powerful of all, muft neceffarily act with decifion and vigour, and by its wife and cautious policy, continue to preferve the wide-extended empire it has acquired, no lefs from the fatal confequences of domeftic diffentions than from the efforts of foreign enemies.

The truth of this obfervation is proved by our own dear-bought experience, and the difappointment given to the hopes we have long cherifhed, and even yet unfortunately too much encourage, of creating a divifion of intereft among the leaders, and in particular of feparating Mahadjee Scindia from the minifter Nana Furnefe.

It is certain a combination of very extraordinary and unforefeen events had, at one period, opened to us a reafonable profpect of obtaining that influence at the court of Poonah which good policy had long fince fuggefted to the Company at home, and induced them to recommend to their fervants in India, as a conftant and leading object, in order to exclude and defeat the intrigues of the French nation.

It is almoft unneceffary to add, that the period to which I allude muft have been that favourable crifis, when Ragonaut Row, brother to the Peifhwa Ballajee Badjerow, after having acted as regent during the minorities of his two nephews, Madhurow and Narrain Row, and upon the demife of the latter, having en-enjoyed the dignity and exercifed the functions of Peifhwa himfelf, was compelled to fly from the machinations of that very party which now governs the Mharatta

ratta ſtate, and to implore the protection and aid of the Engliſh to reſtore him to his native rights.

It is at that period I propoſe to commence my narrative, becauſe it was then that our affairs became ſo intimately blended with Mharatta politics, as to form a leading object in all our future councils and meaſures, and it is to the line of conduct then adopted by the government of Bengal, that we may aſcribe the preſent war with that nation, and of courſe the multiplied misfortunes and ruin with which, in its conſequences, it has already overwhelmed the Britiſh intereſts in India.

Had the Governor General and Council, when they received a clear, and, as it afterwards appeared, unexaggerated account of the ſtate of the war, (wiſely, and in conformity to the wiſhes of the Company, entered into by the government of Bombay in ſupport of Ragonaut Row) choſe to avail themſelves of the favourable opportunity, which their own unimpaired ſtrength, and the comparative weakneſs of the acting adminiſtration at Poonah, ſo fortunately offered them; and inſtead of putting an immediate ſtop to hoſtilities, had they ſhewed the ſmalleſt determination of ſupporting the claims of the unhappy exile, there cannot remain a doubt in the breaſt of any unprejudiced perſon, who has read and conſidered attentively the public records of that period, but that Ragonaut Row, in conjunction with us, would have ſhortly been enabled to dictate terms of ſubmiſſion to his opponents, and that with the re-eſtabliſhment of his authority, all our political objects and wiſhes in the Mharatta ſtate would have been completed.

In proof of this aſſertion, it is only neceſſary to mention the following undoubted fact, "that when the
"treaty

"treaty with Ragoba was concluded by the Bombay
"government, and their troops had joined him in the
"field, the minifters were fo exceedingly alarmed,
"that they fent a vakeel to Bombay to folicit peace,
"on terms the moft advantageous both to Ragoba and
"the Company; but before they had delivered their
"commiffion, which they were prevented fome days
"from doing, on account of the Governor's being in-
"difpofed, letters arrived from the Bengal government,
"difavowing the war, and profeffing a determination
"to make peace; in confequence of which, the vakeel
"changed his tone, haughtily demanding the reftitu-
"tion of Salfette, and the other places of which we
"had taken poffeffion, and the furrender of Ragonaut
"Row into their hands."

It is farther worthy of obfervation, that at the time of our withdrawing the Bombay troops from Ragonaut Row's fupport, his own force confifted of between thirty and forty thoufand men, the greateft confidence and alacrity prevailed throughout the army, in confequence of the fuperiority recently obtained over the minifterial leader, Hurry Punt Forkea, and many of the principal chiefs of the oppofition had given proofs of an inclination to efpoufe the interefts of Ragonaut Row, which they would moft affuredly have followed, if we had difcovered any intention of profecuting the advantages already obtained by our arms, and encouraged them to take fuch a ftep, by affording a fafe and certain afylum againft the dangerous confequences that might otherwife attend it.

Inftead of this, a line of conduct totally different, was unfortunately adopted, and the fentiments of a majority, equally remarkable for the rectitude and integrity of the principles which dictated all their meafures,

fures, as for the impolitic and fatal tendency of many of the meafures themfelves, prevailed in Bengal againft every argument of a juft and wife policy, derived from the long experience and obfervation of the gentlemen who at that time conftituted the minority, and who in the inftance now alluded to, were certainly directed by a perfect knowledge of, and regard to, the interefts of the Company and their country.

The confequence of thefe meafures was fuch as might naturally have been expected. The Mharatta adminiftration, taking advantage of the eager and anxious defire we difcovered for peace, dictated one, upon conditions in every refpect difproportioned to the fuccefs of our arms, and to the fuperior condition we were in at that time to profecute the war.

Inadequate and imperfect as they were, we however acceded to them, and the impatience of the Bengal government to obtain a treaty, did not fuffer them to difcern, that the one concluded by Colonel Upton at Poorunda, March 1ft, 1776, was of fo ambiguous and indeterminate a nature, as to give entire fecurity and fatisfaction to neither party, and to put it in the power of both to renew the war, whenever it might fuit either their intereft or inclination.

The Mharattas in the mean time reaped the moft folid benefits from this treaty. Sunk confiderably as a ftate in that confequence, which before the famous battle of Panniput * they held among the ftates of Hindoftan,

---

* In this remarkable battle, fought little more than twenty years ago, the principal Mahommedan chiefs in Hindoftan, ranged under the banners of the conquering Abdallah Durannee, ftruggled for fuperiority with the Hindoo powers led on by the Mharattas,

Hindoſtan, and which, under the ſhort but vigorous adminiſtration of Madhurow, elder brother to Narrain Row, they were juſt beginning to recover, when his death, and the diſſentions that enſued, joined to the ſuccefsful interpoſition of our arms, plunged them once more into weakneſs and diſtreſs, they required a ſhort peaceful receſs, not only to deliver them from the dangers immediately impending, but to recruit their exhauſted ſtrength, and prepare for future conteſts.

Such a reſpite was peculiarly ſeaſonable to the party which then directed the government, in oppoſition to the claims of Ragonaut Row, becauſe it afforded the leaders of it an opportunity of exerting all their arts to blacken his character and effectually ruin his cauſe; and it is to the good uſe they made of this opportunity, that we may attribute the total diſaffection which afterwards prevailed againſt Ragoba throughout the Decan, and rendered every future effort in his favour inadequate and unſuccefsful; for by delay, always dangerous, and commonly fatal in domeſtic conteſts, the threats and promiſes of the miniſter, joined to the liberality he found it neceſſary to practiſe on many occaſions, had leiſure to operate in their full extent; and thoſe men who entered into the original aſſociation

---

Mharattas, and, after a ſevere and bloody conflict, proved victorious. Soujah ul Dowla diſtinguiſhed himſelf greatly on this occaſion; and on the ſide of the Mhrattas, beſides many leaders of note, and above twenty-five thouſand men, the famous Sudeba, brother to the reigning Peiſhwa, Ballajee Pundit, and his eldeſt ſon, Viſſnaut Row, were unfortunately ſlain. This melancholy event made ſo deep an impreſſion on the mind of the father, as to ſhorten his days, and for a conſiderable period before his diſſolution, he was conſtantly repeating the name of his beloved ſon, and holding imaginary converſations with him.

C againſt

against Ragoba, were not only confirmed in their own enmity, but conscious of the resentment and jealousy which must continue to animate him, should he experience any favourable change of fortune, they felt it impossible to place the smallest confidence in his professions of favour, and promisses of forgiveness, and therefore considered their own destruction as the necessary consequence of his elevation to power.

The character of the man greatly encouraged such an idea, and the apprehension of his vindictive spirit was so great, that even those who were originally well-affected to his interests, and had never taken any active part against him, but who had peaceably acquiesced, or perhaps continued to hold appointments under the new administration, thought it dangerous to risque a change, which must expose them to the effects of his jealousy and suspicion, and became therefore interested in the support and success of his adversaries.

Thus the impolitic and unseasonable treaty, concluded with the Mharattas in March 1776, deprived us of the advantages which were then certainly within our grasp; and by the ruin it brought upon the cause of Ragonaut Row, rendered a future war an object of the greatest difficulty and hazard, and not to be undertaken but upon grounds of expedient and indispensable necessity.

To the misfortune of the Company, their ruling servants in India were not contented with representing merely the disappointment occasioned by this treaty, but they drew such a flattering picture of the unsettled and distracted state of the Mharatta government, and suggested in such lively colours the advantages which we might still be able to reap from their divisions, that, as the " Delenda est Carthago" of the wise Cato was

formerly

formerly the favourite and popular maxim with the ambitious Romans, to pave their way to univerſal empire, in like manner, the ſettlement of the Mharatta ſtate became a fixed and primary object with our leading politicians, both at home and abroad, in order to ſecure an unrivalled dominion in India.

From this circumſtance it happened, that the Court of Directors, deceived by falſe and exaggerated repreſentations, did not give that deciſive and ſalutary check to the diſpoſition of their preſidencies in India, which alone could have prevented a renewal of hoſtilities:— on the contrary, they contented themſelves with ſimply declaring their poſitive intention of ſtrictly adhering to the terms of the treaty made by Colonel Upton, which they, however, acknowledge is not upon the whole ſo agreeable to them as they could wiſh, and feel themſelves at the ſame time compelled, by motives of honour, humanity, and juſtice, to authoriſe a breach of it, by agreeing to the protection given to Ragoba, in direct contradiction to an expreſs article (and no doubt, in the opinion of the Mharatta miniſter, the moſt intereſting and important one) of the treaty.

It was, in fact, impoſſible for the Company to have adopted a different line. To have ſurrendered Ragonaut Row into the hands of his inveterate, his perſonal enemies, would have entailed an indelible ſtain upon the honour and good faith of the nation, and have been juſtly conſidered as a baſe and puſillanimous action, which no proſpect of future advantage could in any reſpect warrant. To perſiſt in affording him protection was an actual breach of treaty, and violation of the public faith ſolemnly pledged for its performance. The alternative appeared at firſt ſight equal, and was certainly a hard one, which required the moſt judicious deliberation, but when maturely weighed, the difficulty of choice foon vaniſhed.

By the former we muſt have rendered ourſelves infamous in the eyes of Hindoſtan and the world, whilſt by the latter, we riſqued little more than offending the Mharattas, and incurring their juſt reſentment and ſuſpicion of our hoſtile intentions.

It is even more than a reaſonable ſuppoſition, that by addreſs and proper management, influenced by a ſincere wiſh on our part to preſerve the peace, we might have been able to ſatiſfy the miniſter, and reconcile him to a meaſure, which it was ſurely our buſineſs to convince him originated ſolely from a regard to our character and dignity as a nation, and not from any views of a nature calculated to ſerve our own ſecret purpoſes hereafter, or to prejudice and deſtroy his authority in the ſtate.

Inſtead of this, the whole of our conduct had evidently a quite oppoſite tendency. We inſiſted, with the moſt minute and ſtudied exactneſs, upon the ſtrict performance of points in themſelves trifling and unimportant, but which, by making the ſubjects of diſcuſſion, we forced into political conſequence, in order to irritate as much as poſſible the minds of the Mharattas. We diſputed about the true meaning of a couple of Perſian words, which, if interpreted to our wiſh, would have added to the Company's annual revenue, the enormous ſum of about ten thouſand pounds ſterling more than the miniſter propoſed to give, in conformity to the ſenſe in which he underſtood them. We alſo peremptorily demanded the diſmiſſion of a perſon belonging to the French nation from the court of Poonah, who, with whatever intentions deputed there, it is evident, and has been ſince fully proved,

did

did not enter into any formal engagements with the minifter, although the latter would have been fully juftified by our conduct relative to Ragoba, and the unfriendly difpofition we fo ftrikingly manifefted, if he had even folicited the alliance and fupport of the French, as a fecurity againft our future hoftile attempts.

On fuch immaterial and ill-founded points did we infift with the minifter, and call his non-compliance a breach of treaty, forgetting how many more important and more juft caufes of complaint he had to exhibit againft us, relative to Ragonaut Row, to the ceffions made by Futty Sing of Chickley, Verriow, &c. &c. and even to the reftitution of Salfette itfelf, which he had been abfolutely taught to expect from the juftice and generofity of the Bengal government.

The apprehenfion (I fhould have faid, the knowledge) of an intended French alliance, has been politically affigned as the principal motive of entering into the war with the Mharattas. The grounds of fuch a belief were, however, altogether fallacious, and I make no fcruple to affert, that the Mharattas never had a thought of any thing more, than maintaining a general good underftanding with the French nation; that they neither wifhed nor attempted to break their alliance with us; and that the hoftilities which immediately followed the facts of which I have been fpeaking, might not only have been prevented by our efforts, but were confequences originating entirely from our own active meafures, abfolutely calculated as well as intended to produce a war.

This affertion naturally excites curiofity to enquire, fince the war on our part is evidently of choice, and

not

not of neceffity, by whofe management and counfel the nation became involved in a conteft, which has proved the fruitful fource of innumerable misfortunes, and has brought us to the very brink of a precipice, beyond which, if we advance a fingle ftep, certain and total ruin muft enfue.

I have already mentioned the diffatisfaction with which the treaty of March 1776 was juftly received both at home and abroad, by all thofe who knew the real fituation of affairs at the time it was concluded, and were fenfible of the advantages we facrificed, without obtaining any adequate benefit or fecurity, in return.

Thefe therefore, it is probable, would readily approve of any fyftem they fuppofed to be calculated to recover that fuperiority; and unfortunately the ruling fervants in India either did not fee themfelves, or chofe not to let their conftituents fee, that the golden opportunity was irrecoverably loft, and that thofe leaders in the Mharatta ftate, who once difcovered an inclination to fupport the interefts of Ragonaut Row, were, for the reafons I have already affigned, become totally averfe from his caufe.

From their partial and exaggerated accounts it unfortunately happened that a latitude of action was left them, of which they did not fail to avail themfelves; and the ambition of a majority on one fide of India co-operated with avarice on the other, to precipitate a rupture, which, if the wife counfels and able policy of Mr. Francis and Mr. Wheeler could have prevailed, muft have been fortunately avoided; nor would Hyder Ally have fince dared to take advantage of a feeble and corrupt adminiftration, to invade the dominions, and ruin the power of the Englifh in the Carnatic.

It is plain, therefore, that the difpofition and fentiments of the Bengal and Bombay prefidencies perfectly correfponded and co-operated on that occafion; but as the latter uniformly confulted with, and acted by the exprefs orders of the former; and as every part of their conduct was authorifed in the moft full and direct manner; as the power of prevention alfo remained with the Bengal government, and as they not only did not exert it, but took an active and zealous part to promote hoftilities, it may furely be advanced, upon every ground of political reafoning and juftice, that Mr. Haftings was the real and refponfible author of the Mharatta war, and that it remains with him to anfwer to the Company and his country for the countlefs train of evils and misfortunes in which it has involved them.

I have thus conducted my narration to the actual breaking out of the war, which I conceive to have been in the early part of the year 1778, when the detachment from Bengal commenced its march (at leaft then fo underftood) to Bombay; for under whatever colour the real intent of this meafure was difguifed, or whatever fpecious arguments were made ufe of at the time to reconcile it to the Mharatta minifter, and to overcome the folid objections brought againft it by the minority, it is evident that Mr. Haftings forefaw, and was prepared for, the confequences; and that, though he affected to exprefs " a reafonable expectation of the " adminiftration at Poonah being alarmed at fo vigo- " rous a meafure, and made to act with more good " faith towards their allies," nothing was farther from his idea, than to prevent hoftilities, which, it plainly appeared from his fubfequent conduct, he was fully bent upon, and determined fhould take place at all events.

The Mharattas themselves, well knowing the difpofition of the Bombay, and, from recent circumftances, fufpicious of that of the Bengal government, could not but behold this propofed acceffion of ftrength to the former at that particular juncture with the moft jealous and anxious eye. They accordingly difcouraged the meafure all in their power, without abfolutely refufing a paffage through their country, and thereby offending the Englifh, which they ftudioufly endeavoured to avoid; and when, notwithftanding their declared difapprobation, the troops perfifted in their march, the minifter certainly confidered fuch conduct as an undoubted proof of our unfriendly intentions, and equal to the moft open and violent act of hoftility.

It was not till the middle of May that the Bengal detachment, confifting of fix battalions of feapoys a company of native artillery, and about eight hundred horfe, (in all near five thoufand men) croffed the river Jumna at Kalpee, a fhort time previous to which a revolution had been effected at Poonah in favour of Moraba Furnefe; and the government of Bombay, who, it fhould be obferved, had neither affifted in bringing it about, nor exerted themfelves vigoroufly in fupporting it after it was accomplifhed, from a belief of this chief's attachment to Ragonaut Row, fent directions to the officer commanding the detachment, to halt where their letter might reach him, until he received their farther orders.

This new adminiftration proved, however, of very fhort duration, and Nana Furnefe, by the timely aid and enterprifing addrefs of Scindea,* foon recovered

his

---

* Nana Furnefe, while in the hands of Moraba, had artfully difguifed his ambitious views under the mafk of the moft fpecious

mode-

his fuperiority, and refumed the reins of government, which he has ever fince continued to guide, while Moraba lingers out a wretched captivity at Ahmednagur, which has been lately made more clofe and rigorous by the difcovery of a plot for his deliverance, to which it is faid the governor of the fortrefs was privy, and has in confequence fuffered death.

I cannot here avoid a fhort digreffion, to obferve how firmly the power of the minifter, Nana Furnefe, feems to be at prefent eftablifhed. Of all the chiefs heretofore leagued with himfelf and rivals in power, and of all thofe who have been at any time fufpected by him, as favourers of the caufe of Ragonaut Row, Moraba is the only perfon remaining to excite the moft diftant jealoufy or apprehenfion. All the reft have either died in prifon, or have purchafed their liberty by the payment of a large fum of money, and contentedly fubmitted to poverty and a private condition.

Hurry Punt Furkea, the general of the ftate, is folely indebted to the minifter for his prefent elevated rank and confequence. He lives with him on the moft confidential footing, and in cafe of his ruin, muft inevitably fhare the fame fate, or fink into total obfcurity.

moderation, and had carried his deep diffimulation fo far, as to declare that he had no other wifh, but to vifit the holy city of Benares, for which purpofe he actually affumed a habit of peculiar piety and devotion, while at the fame time he was fecretly carrying on a correfpondence with Mahadjee Scindea, and fettling with that chief the precife manner and particular hour for apprehending Moraba and refcuing himfelf. This fervice Scindea accordingly performed on the 28th of June, at the head of twenty-five thoufand men, and fecured the perfon of Moraba, whilft Nana laughed at the credulity of his rival, and deridingly told him, that he meant to defer his vifit to Benares a little longer.

D   Scindea,

Scindea, to whom Nana Furnese may be said to owe every thing, has reaped and still enjoys every solid advantage, both with respect to fortune and ambition, which, as the most powerful subject of a great and well-established empire, (and to nothing more must he aspire) he can possibly desire or expect. No change of government will prove beneficial to him; and the degree of jealousy mutually subsisting betwixt himself and Hurry Punt, which Nana, it is probable, sees, and secretly encourages, to render each more immediately dependant upon himself, must at all events prove a sufficient check and obstacle to their forming any designs prejudicial to a person, whose continuance in power they know to be so strictly connected with their own safety and success.

Holkar only remains to be mentioned; and his personal character is an ample security against any mischief which his influence in the state, even if prompted by secret inclination, could possibly effect; for he has all along been directed by Scindea in his political conduct; nor is there any reason to suppose he will venture to embrace a different system.

From the above remarks, and from the farther consideration, that all the other Mharatta chiefs of any weight or consequence are Brahmins, and by their prejudices against Ragonaut Row, no less than by their interested connection with the minister, under whom they enjoy confidence and authority, are of course firmly devoted to his cause, it is assuredly a reasonable opinion, as far as human foresight can reach, to pronounce the present administration of Poonah established upon the firmest and most durable basis, and equally secure from domestic dissentions and internal treachery, as it is from the efforts of foreign enemies, whose dangerous

gerous and enterprifing attacks it has in a late ftriking inftance, by an able, extenfive, and well-concerted fyftem of policy, found means effectually to defeat in the very moment of fuccefs.

The reftoration of Nana Furnefe's authority made it neceffary for the Bombay government to revert once more to their hoftile fyftem. They accordingly fent orders for the advance of the Bengal troops, and relying upon their fupport, they proceeded to contrive the means of oppofing and removing the acting adminiftration at Poonah, which had been the original object of the formation of the detachment, and indeed of all the meafures which they had been purfuing for a confiderable time before, in concert with the Bengal prefidency.

The refolution of the Select Committee of Bombay, for adopting a fpecific plan in favour of Ragoba, was taken the 21ft of July, and communicated to the honourable Governor General and Council, whofe approbation they received the 27th of September following. A formal treaty was then concluded with that chief, bearing date the 24th of November, 1778, and the Bombay forces immediately took the field, in order to conduct him to Poonah, and place him in the regency, according to the agreements mutually made for that purpofe.

Thus far no part of the conduct of the Bombay government appears in any degree reprehenfible. I do not, however, allude to the particular conditions fettled with Ragonaut Row on this occafion. It was, perhaps, in one refpect, fortunate, that the entire failure of the enterprife itfelf prevented them from ever becoming the fubjects of ferious confideration or difcuffion. I fpeak only, at prefent, to the general nature

ture of the plan, which, it muft be acknowledged, was undertaken with the pofitive fanction, concurrence, and, I may fay, knowledge of the Governor General and Council.

How ftrange, then, how inconfiftent, and how contrary to every rule of policy, and even common fenfe, will the conduct of the latter be judged, when it is known, that they were at the fame time fecretly attempting a negociation with Modajee Bofla, the Rajah of Berar, the real object of which they ftudioufly concealed from the knowledge of the Bombay government; and by a refinement in political intrigue heretofore uneffayed, thought to attain a determinate end, by purfuing at one and the fame time two diftinct avenues of action, which pointed to objects diametrically oppofite, and which it was abfolutely impoffible could ever unite, or be in the fmalleft degree reconciled to each other.

In order to explain this bufinefs fully, it is neceffary to recur to the period almoft immediately fubfequent to the revolution at Poonah in favour of Nana Furnefe, when by the vigilance and zeal of the gentlemen who compofed the Secret Committee for managing the Company's affairs in Europe, certain intelligence of a French war was communicated with a fecrecy and difpatch that can fcarcely be credited.

This intelligence did Mr. Haftings make the bafis of his propofal for a plan he had long meditated of an alliance with the Rajah of Berar, the grand object of which involved the fuccefs of a project the moft wild and impracticable that ever entered the mind of a politician. It was in fact altogether chimerical, and in no fhape to be reconciled to the known abilities and political difcernment of him who cherifhed, and has

fince

since continued to indulge it, to such a height of extravagant and infatuated belief, as not to allow the evidence of positive facts which carried conviction to all the world besides, to diminish the confidence he placed in the friendly disposition of the Berar prince, or even totally destroy the hopes he still maintained of raising him to the sovereignty of the Mharatta empire.

The delusion at first imbibed has continued to operate to our prejudice during the whole of the war; and I cannot but consider the proposals for a treaty with the Mharatta administration, transmitted through the channel of Modajee Bosla, in October, 1780, and the late appointment of Mr. Chapman to the court of Naigpore, possessing at the same time authority to negociate with the Mharatta state, as two measures equally weak, impolitic, and destructive of the true interests of the Company, as well as frustrating their ardent desire for peace. But the justice of this remark will be more fully proved in the detail of subsequent transactions. It is sufficient for the present purpose to observe, that even at the period of which I am now speaking, and previous to the full discovery which the government of Bengal might have made of Modajee's real intentions, from the correspondence of Mr. Watherston, who was deputed in December, 1778, to the court of Naigpore by General Goddard, and particularly from a letter addressed to them by the General himself, dated at Burhanpore, February 5, 1779, where, after mentioning the advices he had just received from the Rajah, of the total overthrow of the Bombay forces at Telliagong, the uncertain, contradictory, and at the same time alarming, nature of the dispatches arrived both from the Bombay Committee and their army in the field, and the determination he had formed in consequence,

sequence, of proceeding immediately towards Surat, he gives his opinion of Modajee's aversion to the future prosecution of the proposed project in the following clear and pointed words: " I am induced to be-
" lieve, he (Modajee) would object to my continuing
" in his dominions, because, with the account he has
" written me of the transactions at Poonah, he has
" proposed my returning to Calcutta by such road as
" I shall find most convenient and eligible, without
" making any reference to your expected replies to
" his letters, or to their consequence in favour of his
" views, in concert with your government."

I say, exclusive of the lights derived from the above source, a cool and impartial consideration of the nature of the plan itself would have served to convince any unprejudiced person of its extravagance, and have suggested the impossibility of prevailing upon a wise and discerning court, like that of the then government of Naigpore, to hazard and endanger its future existence as a powerful state, in pursuit of a chimerical scheme of aggrandizement, which, upon every principle of political reasoning and judgment, was surrounded by such great and innumerable difficulties, as to be justly pronounced impracticable.

What excuse, then, can be brought for the Bengal government's wishing to adopt such a scheme, and not only seriously endeavouring to effect it, but doing so at a time when they had reason to believe the presidency of Bombay had actually entered upon the execution of another, under their express sanction and authority, and depended for its success upon the support of the Bengal detachment, supposed to be then on its march to their assistance?

That

That this, however, was the cafe, it is only neceffary to obferve, that the approbation given by the Bengal government to their propofed plan in favour of Ragonaut Row was dated in Auguft, 1778, and the inftructions given to General Goddard, upon the grounds of thofe formerly furnifhed Mr. Elliott, in the November following. That in the preceding month of July, they had briefly communicated Mr. Elliott's miffion to the Bombay Council, but had concealed the particular object of it, relative to an offenfive alliance with Modajee, and his eftablifhment in the Râuge of Settara. That it is true, they then ufed the precaution, in order, as they fay, to prevent any fteps of a contrary tendency on the part of the Bombay prefidency, to requeft " that " they would refrain from forming any engagements " of a nature hoftile to the adminiftration at Poonah, " excepting fuch as might appear abfolutely neceffary " for the defence of their own poffeffions ;" and that even this precaution, vague and inconclufive as it muft appear, was intirely neglected in the letter of approbation above alluded to, which contained only a reftriction " from entering into any engagements with Ragoba " of a tendency hoftile to the government of Berar, " or contrary to fuch as Mr. Elliott might have ap-
" prized them of his having concluded with Modajee " Bofla."

Thus, then, it plainly appears, that the government of Bombay, through the whole of the tranfactions which followed Colonel Upton's treaty in March, 1776, to the formation of the engagements made with Ragoba in November, 1778, were encouraged, fupported, and fully authorifed by the Governor General and Council, who neverthelefs moft unaccountably, I had almoft faid treacheroufly, deferted their plan at the
very

very moment it became ripe for execution, and secretly adopted a new and distinct project, the pursuit of which could not fail, in its consequences, effectually to defeat the success of the enterprise in favour of Ragoba; nor was it till the month of March, 1779, and after the arrival of General Goddard at Bombay, that a copy of Mr. Elliott's original instructions was received by the President and Select Committee, and the nature of the proposed alliance with Modajee Bosla fully explained to them.

Another circumstance deserves mentioning, as it tends farther to display the inconsistency and duplicity of the Bengal government throughout this business in the most striking colours; which is, that on the 15th of October, 1778, they wrote to the presidency of Bombay, generally advising them of the friendly disposition of the Berar Rajah, but acquainting them, that as Mr. Elliott was dead, they proposed to wait for advices from the Rajah before they appointed any other person to succeed him. They at the same time authorise the gentlemen of Bombay to " give orders to the " officer commanding the Bengal detachment, to pro- " ceed forwards in support of the plan for reinstating " Ragoba in the regency, if they think such a step " necessary."

The unfortunate issue of the expedition from Bombay to accomplish that object is too well known to require a description in this place. The malicious exertions of party have operated in secret, and the impressions made by a generous sense of national disgrace and loss, have publicly and powerfully united to load the unhappy actors in that distressful scene with every species of reproach and infamy, and even to plunge them into irremediable ruin.

It

It is not the intention of the author of thefe fheets to join in the popular cry, or to wipe off the odium which has afperfed their characters. It is a fubject he does not mean to difcufs. But juftice as well as humanity generally claims the impartial teftimony of his pen on this occafion; and the enquiring eye of unprejudiced truth will trace the failure of the enterprize to a fource far different from the fuppofed mifconduct of thofe men, who had the immediate management and direction of it.

It will difcover the certain feeds of difappointment in a diftruft and jealoufy which early took place between the two prefidencies, which deftroyed every ground of mutual confidence, and which, by producing open neglect on the one part, and fecret refentment on the other, ultimately defeated the views of both, and ended in the moft fatal and ruinous confequences to the public.

It will fee the Governor General and Council of Bengal prefering a favourite fcheme projected by themfelves, yet, as if confcious of its extravagance and abfurdity, afraid of openly avowing that preference, and at the fame time purfuing fuch unaccountable means, and iffuing orders of fo contradictory a nature, as to perplex, embarrafs, and totally overturn the very plan they were bound by their own inftructions and pofitive promifes to fupport.

It will alfo fee the prefidency of Bombay in their turn, aware of this unlucky predilection, which interfered with their views, ingenioufly contriving to deceive themfelves as well as others into a belief of the ftrength and fufficiency of their caufe, and without encouragement from any partizans of Ragoba, or waiting for the fupport of the Bengal detachment, (which though

though delayed, muſt, they might have been confident, at laſt arrive) precipitately plunging into a conteſt to which they were unequal, and ſacrificing the intereſts of their country to the feelings of reſentment and the dictates of a ſelfiſh and jealous ambition.

Theſe will be the latent cauſes and facts diſcernable by the keen and ſearching eye of truth, and their reality will be confirmed, by obſerving the line of conduct afterwards purſued by both parties. No crimination or enquiry into the behaviour of individuals, but an affected moderation on the part of the Bengal preſidency, which in notorious caſes of public delinquency is ſurely moſt unpardonable, and no accuſation of, or reflection upon, the particular meaſures of the Bombay government, in order to account for, and explain the cauſes of the late miſcarriage, which was certainly due to public juſtice, and abſolutely neceſſary for their own vindication.

In ſhort, a mutual conſciouſneſs of the large ſhare each had contributed to the public misfortunes, made neither party deſirous of too minute an enquiry into the tranſactions which led to them, and they judged it for the common intereſt to adopt a ſyſtem of forbearance and moderation, which they have ſince maintained towards each other with a tolerable degree of temper, but from which it is probable they will now very ſhortly depart.

After the return of the Bombay army from Tilliagong, and the arrival of the Bengal detachment at Surat, on the 25th of February, 1779, an event that, excluſive of any merit derived from it in a political light, reflected equal honour upon the courage and diſcipline of the troops, and the military ſkill and abilities of the officer who commanded and conducted them acroſs the peninfula, the firſt material circumſtance that occurred, was the receipt of a letter from the Governor General and Council, dated the 5th of the fame month, appointing General Goddard their miniſter at the Mharatta court.

The inſtructions that accompanied, were prepared under a probable belief of the enterprife in favour of Ragonaut Row having fucceeded, and were calculated for entering upon a negociation with that chief.

A fituation of affairs in the Mharatta empire, fo widely different from what the Bengal government expected when they drew up the inſtructions, had of courfe rendered them entirely ufelefs and inapplicable when they arrived, and accordingly the General wrote to Bengal, that he fhould defer making known to the adminiſtration at Poonah the commiffion with which he was intruſted, until he could receive farther inſtructions.

I muſt, however, give a fhort extract from the Bengal Council's letter here, as it marks fo ſtrongly their difappointment at the fuppofed fuccefs of a meafure, which, though not of their own formation, they are forced to acknowledge was authorifed by them; and, indeed, the tendency of the letter altogether was fuch, and expreffed fo pointedly their determination of profecuting the plan in favour of Modajee at a future opportunity, that I make no doubt, had even Ragoba been raifed to the government, another revolution muſt fhortly have been attempted.

After acknowledging the receipt of General Goddard's letters from Houffungabad, of the 4th and 6th of January, communicating the failure of his negociation with the Berar Rajah, they proceed as follows:
" We are very much concerned that Modajee Bofla

(28)

"should have so far distrusted the powers with which you were invested, as to suppose that any engagements formed by the President and Council of Bombay, could preclude the accomplishment of a treaty with him, if such had been concluded, and therefore, that he declined to enter into the proposed negociation. If a treaty had been executed by you on the prescribed terms, it would have been our duty to enforce it in preference to any made at Bombay, and to have taken care, that no conditions in which that presidency might have bound itself, should have operated to the prejudice of our engagements. But in the present situation of things, we approve and applaud the prudence and active zeal for the interests of the Company which you have shewn, in the resolution so immediately taken on receipt of the requisition from the President and Select Committee of Bombay, to relinquish the prosecution of the commission which had been especially entrusted to you, and to proceed with the detachment under your command to support the measures, in which that presidency was actually engaged, and in which they had so far committed the safety and prosperity of their own government, and perhaps the general welfare of the Company, as to require every aid that could possibly be given to them.

"As the treaty concluded by the President and Select Committee of Bombay with Ragonaut Row was declared to be made under our sanction and authority, and as we actually did grant our consent to such a treaty on the 17th of August, 1778, we are determined to abide by and support it, notwithstanding the total change which has since taken place in the circumstances under which it was pro-
"posed

" pofed to us, and the new meafures which we have
" ourfelves adopted on the fuppofed failure of thofe
" planned by the prefidency of Bombay."

Speaking of the alliance with Modajee, they ufe the following expreffive words. " However we may be
" reftrained by motives of policy from profecuting
" this meafure, under the circumftances which have
" caufed the fufpenfion of it, we are by no means pre-
" cluded by the terms of the treaty with Ragoba; the
" pretenfion of Bofla to the Râuge or fovereign autho-
" rity of the Mharatta ftate, exifting independently of
" any connections betwixt the Englifh Eaft-India Com-
" pany and Ragoba, and being perfectly reconcileable
" with them."

On the 5th of the fucceeding April, the Governor General and Council having then received authentic accounts of the defeat of the Bombay army, and of the difgraceful convention made at Worgaum with the minifterial leaders for its fafe and unmolefted return, together with the feveral tranfactions fubfequent to that unfortunate event, thought proper to furnifh * General Goddard with frefh credentials, as their minifter at the court of Poonah, and to empower him to negociate a treaty, the exprefs object of which was " to renew or
" confirm that formerly concluded by Colonel Upton,
" provided the Mharattas would previoufly agree to
" recede from the pretenfions they had acquired by the
" late engagements of Meffrs. Carnac and Egerton,
" and agree not to admit any French forces into their
" dominions, or allow that nation to form eftablifh-
" ments on the Mharatta coaft."

* It was at this time he was alfo advanced from the rank of Colonel to that of Brigadier-general, with every flattering encomium and mark of diftinction.

Under

Under thefe reftrictions, and with this latitude of action, excepting that authority was farther granted to relax in fome trifling points relative to Colonel Upton's treaty, which, it is curious to obferve, were once deemed of fo great importance, as to conftitute the declared ground of a rupture betwixt the two States, a negociation was opened by General Goddard at Surat, and carried on with the moft unremitting affiduity and zeal during the months of Auguft, September, and October, 1779; at the expiration of which period, a pofitive anfwer was received from Poonah to the propofals tranfmitted by the General, for the minifter's confideration and acceptance, and in confequence of the determined fpirit of hoftility which dictated it, all farther negociation was immediately broke off, and the Mharatta vakeels returned to their mafter.

It has been ill-naturedly fuggefted, and continues to be the malicious endeavour of thofe, who, upon the illiberal principles of a miftaken policy, think they are rendering a fervice to the Bombay adminiftration, by fixing a large fhare of blame upon the Governor General and Council, becaufe the latter neceffarily took upon themfelves the care and refponfibility, to attribute the failure of General Goddard's negociation to an unreafonable obftinacy and feverity in the demands he was inftructed to make, and to a wanton and ftudied wifh on his part to involve the Company in a war, the management of which would be left to him.

This fufpicion, however, muft be proved to be as falfe as it is ungenerous, when circumftances come to be explained; and candour will not only fimply acquit, but in juftice acknowledge, that every proper effort was ufed to bring about a peace, and that the failure of the negociation, and fubfequent renewal of hoftilities, was occafioned by the influence of the fentiments which then prevailed in the Mharatta councils, and which determined the minifter to reject all overtures for an accommodation, and to put no farther truft in a power, whofe late perfidious breach of faith had proved it to be totally undeferving of a generous confidence, and incapable of a friendly alliance, unlefs where it perfectly fuited with particular views of convenience, or was dictated by neceffity.

In this latter point of view he certainly confidered our advances, and was therefore the more eafily led to prefume, upon his late fuccefs at Telliagong, to hope that the Peifhwa's arms would once more triumph, and prove fuperior to our military exertions.

Add to this, the refentment the minifter muft naturally feel at being fo egregioufly duped by a fham convention on our part, and at the ungrateful return we made for his moderation and mercy, together with the determined enmity we difcovered towards him, in continuing to afford protection to Ragonaut Row, and we fhall then find the true caufe which prolonged the Mharatta war, and which drove Nana Furnefe into an unnatural alliance and confederacy with Hyder Ally. This confederacy, to which Nizam Ally and Modajee Bofla acceded, was formed fo early as the period I am now fpeaking of, and General Goddard gave intelligence of it to the Governor General and Council in the month of September, 1779.

I fhall difmifs the fubject of this negociation by generally obferving, that the fpirit of the Bengal government's inftructions was certainly calculated to promote a juft and honourable peace, and that the actual ftate of circumftances at that time would not have juftified their agreeing to one of a different nature.

It would not, however, be doing juftice to General Goddard, to be totally filent regarding the exertions he ufed to render them effectual, and therefore I fhall give a brief abftract of his conduct.

The vakeels from the Poonah court did not arrive at Surat till the middle of Auguft, previous to which, he had, by every means his fituation afforded, endeavoured to imprefs the minifters with an idea of his pacific and friendly intentions, in protecting and encouraging the fubjects of the Mharatta ftate.

This conduct he perfifted in after the arrival of the vakeels.* In explaining the feveral points of the negociation, he invariably expreffed himfelf in a language the moft moderate, though firm, and in terms which fully proved a fincere defire to become the inftrument of a perfect reconciliation betwixt the two ftates. He wrote to the minifter, accompanying the propofals for peace, that as foon as he had communicated his approbation of them, in order to prevent every avoidable delay, he (the General) would immediately fet out for Poonah; and a confiderable time elapfing without any explicit anfwer being received to the propofitions which had been tranfmitted, he difpatched Lala Nehál

---

* The following extract from the Governor General and Council's letter, dated Sept. 16, 1779, proves the political addrefs and moderation of his conduct: " We obferve with fome " degree of pleafure, the notice taken by the Mharatta govern- " ment, in their letters to you, of the liberal attention which " you had fhewn to the interefts of that ftate, in the protection " given to their aumils in Guzarat againft the irregularities of " Ragoba's dependants, and we recommend a continuation of " the fame kindnefs and moderation in all your conduct to- " wards them."

Chund,

Chund, one of the two Mharatta agents, fully inftructed, and properly encouraged, to his mafter.

This man carried the propofed conditions in writing; nor was it till his return to Surat, with the following pofitive declaration on the part of the minifter, viz. " That he could not make peace with the Englifh, un-
" lefs they delivered up Ragonaut Row into his hands,
" and made immediate reftitution of the ifland of Sal-
" fette," that the General, in obedience to the orders he had received from Bengal, broke off the negociation, and difmiffed the vakeels.

All hopes of peace being thus deftroyed, it became neceffary to prepare for hoftilities, and the General accordingly proceeded to carry into execution, a plan of military operations which he had formed, with the concurrence and approbation of the Select Committee of Bombay; who, in addition to the powers he had received from Bengal, thought proper alfo to delegate to him the authority of their government, and to appoint him their minifter with Futty Sing Row Guicowar, and fuch other chiefs in the Guzerat, as it might be neceffary to engage in our interefts for the more fuccefsful profecution of the war.

It is proper here to obferve, that the general conduct of the war, both in the formation of plans, and in the execution of them, was left to the choice and direction of General Goddard, guided by the advice and information of the Bombay Prefidency; and as it marks the cordial union which at one period fubfifted betwixt them, and the delicacy and moderation which diftinguifhed the General's conduct, under circumftances fo invidious and difgufting, it may not be amifs to tranfcribe the following extract of a letter from the honourable Governor General and Council, dated the

14th of June, 1779. "We obferve with the higheft
"fatisfaction the approbation which the Select Com-
"mittee of Bombay exprefs at your conduct, and the
"ready difpofition which you have fhewn to affift in
"the execution of their defigns. It is with pleafure
"that we have refolved to join with them in recom-
"mending you to the Court of Directors, for the ap-
"pointment of commander in chief at that Prefidency,
"whenever there may be a vacancy," &c.

Although by the efcape of Ragonaut Row from the hands of their enemies in June 1779, and his arrival in the Englifh camp, where General Goddard had judged it for the honour and intereft of the Company to grant him and his family an afylum, and to promife him per- fonal protection in the name and with the fubfequent intire approbation of the Bengal government: I fay, al- though from this circumftance, matters had reverted to the fame ftate in which they were previous to the Tel- liagong expedition, it was not, however, found expe- dient to extend our connection with that unfortunate and unfriended chief beyond the mere affurance of perfonal fafety, or to renew in any fhape the engage- ments which had been formerly entered into with him by the Bombay government.

Fatal experience had already convinced us of the rooted averfion and enmity which prevailed againft him throughout the Mharatta ftate; and that therefore we fhould little grace or ftrengthen our caufe, by uniting it with the affertion of his unpopular and otherwife unfupported claims.

His prefence in the cafe of a rupture with the Poo- nah adminiftration, which had in fpite of every effort proved unavoidable, was certainly of very beneficial confequence, in augmenting the fears of our enemies,

and

and arming us with the means of injuring them more essentially if we proved successful, or of accommodating our difference with the greater ease and advantage, should we at any time wish to bring the war to a termination.

From all these considerations, it was left to time and future circumstances to determine the extent of our benefits to Ragonaut Row; and in the intermediate space, we entered upon the war avowedly as principals, compelled to it by the refusal of the Mharatta minister to accept of the just and reasonable conditions of peace we had proposed to him, which rendered hostilities on our part an act of self-preservation and defence.

The inferior estimation in which the cause of Ragoba was necessarily held, and the little influence it had upon the future operations of the war, might almost render an apology requisite for having suffered it to engage so much present attention: but the best excuse to be made is, that I shall here take leave of him, and that most probably his name will not once occur during the remainder of this narrative.

On the first of January, 1780, the army under General Goddard, reinforced by a small detachment of Bombay troops, commanded by Lieutenant-colonel Hartley, crossed the river Tappy, on its route to Guzerat.

It had been resolved to commence the campaign with the settlement of that province, and the General lost no time in accomplishing an object, which, besides the great importance of it to the general success of the war, it was particularly necessary should be finally adjusted previous to the arrival of the Mharatta forces in the neighbourhood, lest their presence should intimidate,

date, and fix decidedly in the Peiſhwa's intereſt, Futty Sing Guicowar, whoſe inclination at the beſt could only be ſuppoſed to be wavering ; and we ſhould by that means be conſtrained to confine our operations to the oppoſition of their united ſtrength, under every poſſible diſadvantage, and without any acquiſition of revenue or improvement of reſource whatever.

I have already premiſed, that it is not my intention to ſwell this narrative, by a minute deſcription and detail of military operations ; but it is with no ſmall reluctance and regret that I muſt on the preſent occaſion decline a taſk, which, from the various proofs it affords of ſkilful conduct in the commander, and of diſciplined valour in the troops, would ſo pleaſingly gratify my private feelings, and allow ſuch ample ſcope to animated language, and all the force of nervous eloquence : juſtice, however, requires that I ſhould generally bear teſtimony to a merit ſo diſtinguiſhed ; and while I mention the many and ſtriking advantages derived to the Company by the operations of this campaign, I cannot help celebrating the able exertions and gallant ſpirit of thoſe, by whoſe united labours and perſeverance they were acquired.

The province of Guzerat could only be ſettled by the two following modes, either by a union of intereſts with Futty Sing, or by forcibly wreſting it out of his hands.

Every idea of reaſon and good policy dictated the former, if it could poſſibly be effected. Upon the eve of engaging in a war with the moſt powerful ſtate in Hindoſtan, and unſupported by any friend or ally, nay, even ſuſpicious of the deſigns of thoſe princes who then profeſſed a neutrality, it ſurely was a point of the

firſt

first confideration, to conciliate and attach Futty Sing to our caufe, fince by fo doing we fecured to ourfelves the immediate poffeffion of a confiderable track of country, and, as it has fince proved, the unmolefted poffeffion of its revenue; an object at that time abfolutely effential for enabling us to enter upon hoftilities with vigour and effect; whereas, if Futty Sing had continued inimical to us, no prefent provifion could poffibly have been made for the future profecution of the war; the province of Guzerat muft have been totally defolated and deftroyed, and even fuch parts of it as we might have been able to poffefs ourfelves of, muft have been expofed to the conftant inroads and ravages of a depredatory enemy. Under the full conviction of thefe felf-evident truths, the General was himfelf exceedingly defirous, and had it in charge from the Select Committee of Bombay, to adjuft amicably with Futty Sing the fettlement of the country, and to render him, if poffible, a ferviceable ally to the Company.

The general character of the man, and the very ftrong prejudices entertained againft him by fome individuals at Bombay, who by a ftrange abufe and perverfion of juftice, chofe to ftigmatize him with the perfidious ftains which, in reafon ought to have fullied the Englifh name, for their treacherous conduct towards him on a former occafion, naturally excited in the mind of the General the ftrongeft doubts and apprehenfions, of the little confidence that could be placed in any promifes or declarations, however fpecious and friendly in appearance, which the Rajah might be induced to make, in order to preferve himfelf from the ruin which then threatened to overwhelm him.

The

The fears of meeting with a treatment fimilar to what he had before experienced,* might alfo make Futty Sing on his part doubtful and fufpicious of our proffered friendfhip; and thefe confiderations, joined to the dread of the Mharatta power, and of the punifhment their vengeance would certainly inflict, feemed to create innumerable difficulties and obftacles to the attainment of a friendly, fincere, and permanent connection betwixt the Company and that chief.

Thefe unpromifing circumftances, however, only ferved to encreafe the General's folicitude and ardour to accomplifh an object of fuch importance, and fo effential to the fuccefsful profecution of the war. He applied himfelf, therefore, to it with an earneft affiduity and zeal, that fully proved the difinterefted fpirit which governed his actions, and taught him to prefer the confcious fatisfaction of procuring a folid and certain benefit to the public, to the falfe glare of a narrow private ambition, or the feducing charms of a rapacious avarice, both of which, the exclufive conqueft of Guzerat and the ruin of Futty Sing would have gratified in their fulleft extent.

Senfible of the good effects which the rapid movements and approach of the army would produce upon

---

* In the year 1775, when the Bombay forces were in the field, in fupport of Ragonaut Row's pretenfions, Futty Sing, after a long negociation through the mediation of the Englifh commander, and under the faith of the Company, was prevailed upon to rifque an interview, when he was forcibly made prifoner by Ragoba, compelled to agree to the payment of a large fum of money, and not fuffered to return to his capital of Baroda, until he had fent for his daughter, a child of fix or feven years of age, and delivered her up as a fecurity for the performance of the engagements violently extorted from him.

Futty

Futty Sing's counfels, the General left the banks of the river Tappy on the 5th of January, and on the 15th croffed the Nerbuddah at Bowapone-Gaut, where he was joined by fome battering cannon and ftores from Baroche, a place of confiderable ftrength and commerce, upon the northern bank of the fame river, and governed by a chief and council under the Bombay Prefidency. On the 19th the army reached Dubhoy, a confiderable walled town belonging to the Mharattas, which the garrifon abandoned the night after the troops arrived before it.

The negociation with Futty Sing had been carried on, without interrupting the progrefs of the march, through the means of vakeels on his part, that paffed to and from the camp; and by the influence of a moderation that does the General infinite honour, joined to the greateft perfeverance and addrefs, the Rajah was at length won over to our views, and agreed to an alliance with the Company upon the terms propofed to him.

The treaty was finally concluded on the 26th of January, at a village called Condeala, about four or five miles from Baroda, Futty Sing's capital, and half way betwixt the latter and our encampment.

By this treaty, the peace and tranquillity of Guzerat was fecured upon the moft firm and folid bafis, an immediate refource of revenue was provided, and that in a manner the leaft expenfive and hazardous to the Company; and the certain and fpeedy fettlement of the province, gave us leifure to turn our arms to new and more neceffary, though, perhaps, lefs beneficial conquefts.

It was with the utmoft vifible and natural reluctance, that Futty Sing was prevailed upon to accept of the

country

country to be conquered from the Mharattas, north of rhe river Myhie, in exchange for an equal proportion of lands to the fouthward; nor is this unwillingnefs on his part to be wondered at, fince, although by uniting his poffeffions in one regular and connected chain, he would be a fimilar gainer with ourfelves, and although the revenues of the country to be mutually exchanged, differed very little in their amount, the real and intrinfic value of the lands could bear no manner of comparifon; and in lieu of a territory, fertile, well cultivated, and to be collected at little or no expence, we put him in poffeffion of a track, it is true, more extenfive, but wild and without culture, inhabited by a fierce and unruly people, and conftantly expofed to the ravages of a plundering banditti, which rendered the maintenance of a confiderable military force at all times requifite, to preferve the tranquillity of the country, and to enforce the collections.

Before I purfue my narrative, it may not be improper to give a brief account of the Guzerat province, and an hiftorical account of the Guicowar family, who poffefs the greateft part of it, from their original founder, Pillajee. This man was grandfather to the prefent reigning prince, and being a very warlike and able chief, attended Sahoo, Rajah of Setterah, in his wars, and obtained, as a reward for his fervices, the province of Guzerat, the greateft part of which he had himfelf conquered from the Mahommedan princes, who at that time governed it in the name of the Mogul emperors.

This rich and extenfive kingdom, for as fuch it has ever been diftinguifhed in the hiftories of the eaft, was conferred upon Pillajee in jaghire, but by a more full and independent tenure than is ufually granted to the jaghire officers amongft the Mharattas.

After

After his death, his son Damajee succeeded, and upon some differences he had with the Mharatta government, was prevailed upon to repair to Poonah, in order to accommodate them, when he was treacherously made prisoner, and compelled to agree to a partition of country with the Peishwa, and to enter into such engagements as were dictated to him, before he could obtain his release.

From that period, the administration at Poonah found means to interfere more immediately in the settlement and government of the province, and the Mharatta forces, under Ragonaut Row, in conjunction with those of Damajee, laid siege, but without success, to the capital Ahmedabad; nor was it wrested from the possession of the Mussulmans so much by superior foreign force, as it was at last betrayed into the hands of the confederates by domestic treason and treachery.

After the demise of Damajee, Futty Sing succeeded, in preference to his elder brother Seajee, who, being disordered in his intellects, was judged incapable of governing. This unfortunate chief resides contentedly at Soan Ghur, a fort belonging to the family, where he is treated with every mark of attention, and has liberty to amuse himself in those innocent pursuits, which his insanity, perfectly inoffensive in its nature, constitutes the only objects and employment of his life.

Gouind Row, another son of Damajee, but by a different mother, though younger than Futty Sing, lays claim to the succession, under pretext of the preferable right which the offspring of the lawful wife possesses over that of the favourite concubine. This distinction, however, is contrary to nature, and the established customs of the east, and Futty Sing has been formally acknowledged by the Poonah durbar, and received the inveftiture of his authority from the nominal Rajah of Setterah.

Until the time of Aurungzebe, and while the Mogul empire continued to flourifh, Guzerat was efteemed one of the moft opulent provinces dependant upon it. It is difficult to conceive a more intire revolution than what has fince taken place. The imbecility of fucceeding monarchs, confpiracies and civil wars in the centre of the empire, and a total relaxation, and decay of vigour, through all the remote and extended provinces of it, univerfally encouraged the viceroys to affert an independence in their refpective governments, nor was the Soubah of Guzerat more difpofed to give proofs of attachment and loyalty than the reft.

This feparation and difmemberment of the empire, proved moft favourable to invaders, who attacked, and with eafe poffeffed themfelves of the divided provinces; and it was about this time that the Mharattas broke forth from the mountains of the Decan, and, fpreading flaughter and defolation wherever they directed their deftructive fteps, terrified and fubdued the effeminate and degenerated defcendants of thofe Mahommedan conquerors, who had themfelves fo courageoufly eftablifhed their empire in Hindoftan, by the edge of the fword, and the terror of their arms.

Some of them, unable to ftem the torrent, abandoned every thing to its rage; and others, fatisfied with a temporary relief, and the indulgence of prefent eafe, attempted to divert its courfe, by the payment of large fums of money, or ceffions of territory.

The province of Guzerat, as has been already obferved, foon fell into their hands. With the lofs of
the

the capital Ahmedabad, the Mogul authority became totally annihilated, and the defcendants of the Nawâb Cummaul ul dien, the family which was then difpoffeffed of government, now refide in obfcurity upon a fmall jaghire, allowed them in the neighbourhood of Puttan, under the protection and jealous vigilance of Futty Sing.

The only veftiges of the Muffelman dominion which now remain, are Surat and Cambait, the former fituated towards the mouth of the river Tappy, and the latter on that of the Myhie. Thefe places are poffeffed by their refpective Mahommedan governors, or, as they ftile themfelves, Nawâbs, but their authority is confined within the walls, and even the fcanty revenue of this circumfcribed extent, they fhare with the Mharattas, who receive a fixed and very confiderable proportion.

Befides the two large rivers above mentioned, this province is alfo watered by a third, the Nerbuddah, which rifes in the hills of Boghilhund, and, after running a weftern courfe of about one thoufand miles, through the rich provinces of Malwa, Chandeifh, and Guzerat, empties itfelf into the gulph of Cambait, a little below the town of Baroche, which was conquered by the Englifh from its Navâb a few years ago.

A fituation fo favourable for commerce could not poffibly be overlooked, and we accordingly find, that this province, and efpecially the town of Surat, has always carried on a moft extenfive and advantageous trade, and was formerly confidered as the grand emporium of the Mogul's dominions, fupplying the moft interiour and remote corners of them with every ufeful commodity, nay, even with every fuperfluity and luxury of life, which the hand of foreign invention or induſtry could contrive or produce.

Its own fertility, ariſing from the nature and ſituation of the ſoil, being a low flat land, and interſected with many ſmaller ſtreams, beſides thoſe large rivers already mentioned, enabled it to export great quantities of cotton, indigo, wheat and other grains; and the improved ſtate of its manufactures amply ſupplied articles for foreign markets, in exchange for the valuable productions purchaſed from them.

I ſhall finiſh this digreſſion with a ſhort account of the city of Ahmedabad, which has long been eſteemed as the capital of the province. It is ſituated upon the eaſt bank of the Sabremetty Nuddy, a pleaſant, wholeſome, and conſtant, though ſmall ſtream, that runs into the Myhie, and it was originally founded by Shaw Ahmed, King of Guzerat, who flouriſhed near four centuries ago. The walls, which ſtill remain, are about ſix miles in circumference, and there is a very wide and deep ditch carried all round. Beſides this ditch, new works have been ſince conſtructed, where the original defences, either from decay or ſituation, were judged inſufficient; and upon the whole, it may be pronounced a very ſtrong and formidable place, eſpecially when garriſoned, as it was at the time when General Goddard beſieged it, by about ſix thouſand Arab and Sindy foot and two thouſand horſe.

There are twelve gateways, by which you paſs in and out of the city; and the extenſive circuit of the walls, particularly at theſe gateways, appears to have been ornamented, at regular diſtances, with towers and cupolas, which in the days of its ſplendour, muſt have equally contributed to the magnificence and ſtrength of the place. Within the city, and upon the

bank

bank of the river, is an extenfive enclofure, called the Budder, which was formerly the royal refidence : it has been ftrongly fortified, and entirely commands the principal bazars, courts of juftice, and ftreets where the palaces of the chief nobles were fituated. At prefent, fo much is this city decayed, and fallen from its original flourifhing condition, that not more than a quarter of the fpace within the walls is inhabited, whereas, from infallible veftiges, and ruins regularly to be traced, the fuburbs muft formerly have extended beyond them to the diftance of three miles round.

Ahmedabad is the Mahommedan capital of Guzerat, the work of Ahmed and his fucceffors, who enlarged and beautified it out of the ruins of the ancient Hindoo cities Narwalla and Chappaneer. Baroche and Puttan, the latter of which is, I believe, a more modern name for Narwalla, are alfo of great antiquity ; but of all thefe, little more than the name exifts at prefent; and the Guicowar capital is called Baroda, recently founded upon the banks of the Bifwamuntry Nuddy, and fituated betwixt the Myhie and Nerbuddah, about twelve miles fouth of the former.

In Ahmedabad is ftill to be feen the mofque and tomb of Ahmed, its founder, built entirely of ftone and marble. Great tafte, fkill, and expence, muft have been exerted on thefe ftructures, which are curious and magnificent, and remain perfect and uninjured by the ruthlefs hand of all-deftroying time.

Many fuperb ruins, both within and without the walls, merit a particular defcription, but I have already digreffed fufficiently, and fhall now return to the fubject of my narrative, after obferving, that Guzerat continued to be governed by a fucceffion of its own kings, until the reign of Acbar, when it was finally fubjected, subjected, and made a province of the Mogul empire, the wretched fate of which it afterward shared, as has been already described.

In conformity to the engagements made with Futty Sing, for putting him in immediate possession of the Mharatta share of the country, north of the Myhie, the army marched from the neighbourhood of Baroda, and arriving before Ahmedabad the 10th of February, upon a refusal of the governor, on the part of the Peishwa, to surrender, besieged and stormed it the 15th in the morning. It was carried after a gallant and desperate resistance, and about four hundred of the enemy were killed in the assault. Most of these fell in the ditch and one of the gateways, where, endeavouring to escape into the town as our grenadiers advanced, they were stopped by the narrowness of the passage and wicket, and falling one upon another, crowded together in a heap, their ammunition blowing up in their cartouch boxes, and every man perishing before relief could be given.

The troops distinguished themselves by every proof of discipline and humanity, injuring no person they found in the place unarmed, and in the fury of attack, sparing even many who laid down their arms and submitted. The prisoners, amongst whom were some Arab Jemedars, were treated with the greatest clementy, and those that were wounded, received into our hospital, humanely taken care of, and afterwards re-eased [*].

On

---

[*] A circumstance similar to the following, must give more heartfelt pleasure to a humane and liberal mind, than the most splendid triumphs of victory; " an officer of the Bombay establishment,

On the 26th of February, Futty Sing was formally put in poffeffion of Ahmedabad, and the fettlement of the Guzerat perfected, and its future tranquillity effectually fecured, in lefs than two months from putting the troops in motion.

This acquifition was by no means of the value or importance to Futty Sing, which, from the reputation of its being the capital, one would be led to fuppofe. A confiderable part of its revenue, the whole of which did not exceed three lacks, had been before received by him, and of the collections of the country, north of the Myhie, more than two-thirds had always belonged to the Guicowar; fo that, in fact, we did little elfe than put him in poffeffion of his own country, and this he was to maintain and defend in future, at the expence of a garrifon which had before been paid by the Peifhwa. The attainment of Ahmedabad was, befides, not the object of Futty Sing's wifh: on the contrary, he was totally averfe to it, and to the whole of the propofed partition of territory, which included that city in his fhare.

It became, therefore, an object of political confideration, to gild the pill we had thus forced him to fwallow, and make it as palatable as poffible; accordingly, General Goddard exerted himfelf, to render the real as well as ideal value of the place as important in Futty Sing's eyes as he could. For the reafons already men-

blifhment, who belonged to a fmall party of fepoys, which was employed, foon after the ftorm of Ahmedabad, in the Concar, and had been defeated, fell into the hands of the Mharattas, and by the influence of an Arab Jemedar, who declared his motive for interceding was, in grateful acknowledgement of the humane treatment his countrymen had met with from General Goddard, obtained his liberty, and returned to Bombay."

tioned,

tioned, he found it as impoffible to give up the city to plunder, as it would have been unjuft and impolitic to infift upon the Rajah's ranfoming it, by the payment of a fum of money to the troops; and he therefore ufed every precaution to prevent a general pillage, in which their good conduct and difcipline fortunately enabled him to fucceed; but his regard for their interefts, and defire of rewarding their valour, muft have made him afterwards not forry to learn, that a partial prize had fallen to their fhare; and to this circumftance he found means to reconcile Futty Sing, although many, and no doubt exaggerated complaints, were daily made; and one merchant in the city eftimated his own lofs at above fifty thoufand rupees. It is proper here to mention, that the greateft part of the property belonging to the inhabitants had been conveyed away to places of fecurity previous to the fiege, and almoft the whole of the little that remained, was the property of people connected with or immediately dependent upon the Guicowar.

Previous to, and during the fiege of Ahmedabad, accounts were daily brought of the great military preparations making at Poonah, and it was foon known that Scindia and Holkar had defcended the gauts with a large army, and advanced towards Baroda, Futty Sing's capital. General Goddard put the troops in motion as expeditioufly as poffible, and leaving Ahmedabad the 2d of March, croffed the Myhie the 6th, and encamped about two miles from Baroda, on the Bifwamuntry Nuddy the 8th.

Scindia and Holkar, with their whole force, had moved off to the eaftward, about twelve or fourteen miles from Baroda, and about the fame diftance from

Powan

Powan Ghur,* a very strong fortress belonging to Scindia, situated upon an exceeding high and almost inaccessible mountain, and separating the two provinces of Malwa and Guzerat. Their united force consisted of at least forty thousand men, most of which were horse, and they had with them a few light pieces of cannon only, having sent away all of a larger size, as well as every species of heavy baggage which could encumber or retard the celerity of their motions.

On the 9th, Messrs. Farmer and Stewart, who had been left with Mahadjee Scindia, as hostages for the faithful performance of the convention of Worgaum, arrived in camp with letters from that chief and Holkar, generally expressive of their friendly sentiments, and of the inclination of the Mharattas to live upon terms of amity with the English; as a proof of which, they had given the above gentlemen their dismission, and instructed them, in conjunction with Abajee Shabajee, to make a full representation of matters to General Goddard.

A conduct so promising and friendly in appearance, excited the most sanguine expectations of soon effecting a peace with the Mharatta State, or, at least, of bringing about some separate agreement with Mahadjee Scindia, which might be productive of the most important benefits to the Company, in the final settlement of their disputes with that nation. It was, therefore, matter of the greatest concern to the General, to see his hopes ultimately disappointed, and all his efforts for that desirable end unluckily defeated.

* The ancient city of Chappaneer stood at the foot of this mountain, and a small town still exists, under the same name, and upon the same spot, which is subject to Scindia.

He endeavoured, by every affurance and argument in his power, to imprefs the mind of Scindia with a belief of the fincere wifh of the Englifh for peace, and of the particular fentiments of regard they entertained for himfelf, of which they were ready to give the moft ftrong and convincing proofs.

He fuggefted fome conditions mutually beneficial, on which they were defirous of uniting with him, in fettling the adminiftration of the empire upon a proper and folid bafis, and failing in this attempt of feparating Scindia from the minifter Nana Furnefe, for which every opening was given, he alfo pointed out fuch terms in an alliance with the prefent government, as the Englifh had a right, founded both in juftice and reafon, to expect, and were ready to accede to.

A very few days, however, fully convinced the General of the inefficacy of his own endeavours, and of the infincerity of Scindia's profeffions. Abajee Shabajee returned with propofals from his mafter, which pofitively proved his intimate connection with Nana Furnefe, and were, indeed, of a nature, if poffible, more difgraceful than thofe before made by the minifter himfelf, requiring the furrender of Ragoba's perfon into his hands, and alfo of his fon Badjerow, the former of whom was to refide at Jancy, upon the allowance Scindia had before fettled for his fubfiftence, and to relinquifh all fhare in the adminiftration, which was in future to be conducted by Scindia, in the name of Badjerow, upon whom the appointment of Dewan to the Peifhwa Madhurow Narain fhould be conferred. No exprefs advantage was propofed to be ftipulated for the Englifh in return for thefe conceffions: on the contrary, Scindia meant to have it underftood, that they were to adhere to the engagements made at Worgaum.

Upon

Upon the whole, it plainly appeared, that Scindia was not in reality fo amicably difpofed, as his behaviour refpecting Meffrs. Farmer and Stewart gave room to conjecture; or that, if he was defirous of peace, there did not exift any reafonable hope of his intention to conclude a treaty, but upon terms that were judged difhonourable previous to the campaign, and which in the midft of our prefent fuccefs would have been deemed highly inadequate and difgraceful.

Thus ended the negociation with Scindia, and though the General, towards the clofe of the campaign, and after the fuperiority of our arms over the Mharattas had been repeatedly afferted, availed himfelf of an opportunity of fome indirect overtures made by Scindia through Futty Sing, to renew the negociation, this fecond attempt proved equally unfuccefsful with the former.

The military operations, after the return of the army from Ahmedabad, were confined, on the part of Scindia, to a determined fyftem of avoiding an engagement, and on that of the Englifh, to every poffible exertion to induce him to alter his refolution.

For this purpofe, the General twice advanced with the whole army, and encamped upon the ground which Scindia had occupied, and from which he had precipitately retired as we advanced. A third time, with a part of the army only, viz. two hundred European infantry, ten companies of grenadier fepoys, two Bengal and one Bombay battalion, two twelve and ten fixpounder pieces of artillery, and about feven or eight hundred horfe, he formed and attempted a plan of furprizing the enemy's camp. Their vigilance and exceffive caution, however, prevented his advancing undifcovered beyond their grand guard of fix thoufand men, which was near two miles from the main army; and when he reached the encampment after day-light, he found the whole drawn up ready for action.

This appearance encouraged a hope, that the important moment at last arrived, when the enemy, presuming upon their numbers, would avail themselves of the opportunity which offered, of contending with only a part of our force, and stand the decision of a battle; but this hope proved fallacious, and after a few brisk though partial skirmishes, the Mharattas entirely abandoned the field to the conquerors, who remained upon it about two hours, and then returned without loss, to their own camp.

These signal triumphs most strikingly evinced the superiority of our arms, and wiped off the stain they had contracted from the late unlucky disaster at Worgaum. They were, besides, the only successes to be gained over an enemy who would not fight, and who, it is probable, wished for nothing more than to draw us on beyond the proper line of our policy, and the defence of our new conquests, to an unprofitable pursuit of his army into the Malwa province; which, besides exposing our valuable acquisitions in Guzerat, would also have endangered the safety of the presidency of Bombay itself, at this time threatened with an attack from the French; and even admitting our endeavours to have been so far successful, as that our arms had penetrated to Ugein Scindia's capital, they could not possibly have produced any benefit at all proportioned to the risque, or decisive towards terminating the war.

The two armies continued on the confines of Malwa and Guzerat until the month of May, when they separated, on account of the approaching monsoon, Scindia

dia marching off to Ugein, and the Englifh returning to Surat, where they arrived the beginning of June.

It would be unjuſt not to mention the particular fervices of Major John Forbes and Captain John Campbell, the former of whom furprifed and defeated a confiderable party of the enemy under one of their principal leaders; and the latter, who commanded two battalions of Bengal fepoys upon a foraging party, being attacked at the diftance of at leaft ten miles from camp, by near fifteen thoufand of Scindia's beft horfe, after killing a confiderable number, forced the reft to retire, and faved not only his party, but brought the forage he had collected fafe to camp.

I fhall conclude this general fketch of the Guzerat campaign, with a fhort teftimony to the merit and gallantry of Lieutenant Welfh, who commanded a corps of three hundred Mogul cavalry, and was detached with that corps, and one battalion of fepoys, to furprife and beat up the quarters of Gunnefe Punt, one of the minifterial chiefs, who with about fix thoufand men infefted the neighbourhood of Surat.

The diftance was about fifty miles, and Lieutenant Welfh had moved with fuch fecrefy and rapidity, that Gunnefe Punt was unapprifed of his approach. He contrived fo as to reach the encampment early in the morning; but perceiving the day would foon break, he ordered the infantry and guns to follow as expeditioufly as poffible, and putting himfelf at the head of the cavalry only, rufhed forward into the midft of the enemy, who, terrified by the impetuofity of an affault fo fudden and unexpected, fled on all fides, and left their guns and baggage a prize to the victors.

This gallant enterprife was fucceeded by the furrender of Parneiro, a fort built upon an high hill, and from its fituation, if properly defended, capable of defying the moft formidable force. The acquifition of this, with the fmaller forts in its vicinity, which Lieutenant Welfh alfo took, entirely completed the conqueft of the Guzerat province, of which Parneiro may be termed the fouthern limit.

Previous to his marching againft this place, Lieutenant Welfh received a fmall reinforcement of fepoys, with battering cannon and ftores, from Mr. Boddam, chief of Surat, whofe name I fhould be unpardonable to mention, without bearing teftimony at the fame time to his zeal for the interefts of the Company, which is ever active, and has confpicuoufly diftinguifhed itfelf on various occafions; nor is he himfelf lefs remarkable for the integrity and difintereftednefs of his public character, than for his many private virtues and amiable qualifications.

Thus terminated the firft campaign of the Mharatta war; and General Goddard, befides the confcious fatisfaction of having uniformly fucceeded in every attempt he made againft the enemy, and of having put the Company in poffeffion of a territory yielding an annual revenue of thirty lacks of rupees, had a farther gratification, not the leaft pleafing to a generous mind, of receiving the moft full and flattering teftimonies from the government of Bengal, of their approbation of every part of his conduct, and the high fenfe they entertained of his fervices to the Company.

During the monfoon of 1780, nothing material occurred, except the important conqueft of Gualior, atchieved by Major Popham, who carried it in the moft enterprifing and gallant manner, and by a fkilful and well concerted ftratagem, that does the higheft honour to his military talents and abilities.

In

In the preceding month of November, Major Popham had received the command of two thoufand drafts, intended to reinforce General Goddard's army, but from various caufes, principally from the danger of attempting to crofs the peninfula with fo fmall a force, the defign was dropped, and a new plan adopted by the Governor General, for making a diverfion in favour of the general operations of the war from the country of the Gohud Ranna, which fhould, in its confequences, involve a combination of the feveral Hindoo princes, interfperfed through the province of Ajmeer, and to the northward of Malwa.

An attempt was accordingly made to negociate with thofe petty chiefs, which unfortunately did not fucceed in any adequate or ufeful degree ; and the political as well as military operations of that quarter, were confined to an alliance with the Ranna of Gohud, and the recovery of his country from the Mharattas.

It was in the execution of this fervice that Major Popham fignalized himfelf, and made the Company's name feared and refpected throughout Hindoftan, by planting the Britifh colours upon the walls of Gualior, a fortrefs which had for ages been deemed impregnable, and where, as in a fecure and inacceffible afylum, the Mogul emperors, in the days of their magnificence and power, had always confined the vanquifhed rivals of their greatnefs, and other eminent prifoners of ftate.

No means of reconciliation with the Mharattas could be found during the rainy feafon of the year 1780, and accordingly a renewal of hoftilities became neceffary.

After providing for the prefervation and fecurity of our acquifitions in Guzerat, the defence of which was committed to a detachment of our own troops, and a proportion of horfe to be furnifhed by our ally, Futty Sing,

Sing, the army marched from Surat the 16th of October, and arrived before Baffein about the middle of November. The battering cannon and ftores were landed with all expedition, and the fiege carried on with fuch unremitting vigour and alacrity, that on the 11th of December, a practicable breach being made, the garrifon, confifting of at leaft fix thoufand men, capitulated and laid down their arms.

Thus by the bravery and good conduct of their troops, was the Company, in the very commencement of the fecond campaign, put in poffeffion of a place, which had been long the object of their ardent wifhes and moft eager folicitude, and which, in the treaty made with Ragonaut Row in 1778, by the Bombay government, had been deemed of fo great importance, as to conftitute the moft material article ftipulated with him in behalf of the Englifh, for invefting him with the regency and entire adminiftration of the Mharatta empire.

The conqueft of Baffein was foon followed by the furrender of Amoll, a fmall, though from its fituation very tenable fort, upon an ifland about one thoufand fix hundred yards diftant from that of Baffein, and whofe poffeffion is abfolutely requifite to fecure the unmolefted enjoyment of Baffein itfelf. The garrifons of Tarrapore, Danou, and other forts, fituated along the fea coaft of the Concan, thought proper to follow the fame example; and at the end of the year 1780, the Englifh, to the conqueft of Guzerat, had added that of the largeft and moft valuable part of the Concan, and were actually mafters of an extent of fea coaft from Cambait to the mouth of the Pen river, which empties itfelf into Bombay harbour, of above three hundred miles.

Thus

Thus far we have conducted the Mharatta war, and from a contemplation of the paſt, ſo far from diſcovering any cauſe of regret for having commenced it, we ſhould be led to entertain the moſt reaſonable and well-grounded expectation, of being ſhortly able to bring it to a glorious and ſucceſsful termination; ſince beſides the conqueſts already made, we actually enjoyed, at the period above mentioned, means for its proſecution infinitely ſuperior to what we originally poſſeſſed, or could have even hoped to acquire in ſo ſhort a time from our own ſingle and unaſſiſted efforts.

Various cauſes, however, unfortunately contributed to diſappoint this hope, the principal of which I acknowledge to have been the breaking out of the war with Hyder Ally Chawn, and the great and unexampled ſucceſs of his arms in the Carnatic. I muſt alſo be of opinion, that the meaſures adopted for bringing about an accommodation were in their nature of ſo impolitic and dangerous a tendency, as to throw obſtacles in the way of it, and by the eagerneſs and anxiety they betrayed, actually defeated the purpoſe they were intended to attain.

I ſhall have frequent occaſion in the courſe of my narrative to elucidate this latter obſervation. I ſhall, therefore, at preſent confine myſelf to a deſcription of the immediate effects of Hyder's unlucky interference, previous to which a ſhort digreſſion ſeems neceſſary for clearly comprehending the ſubject.

Although the controling powers veſted in the Governor General and Council, were certainly intended by the wiſdom of the legiſlature, to guard againſt the deſtructive conſequences, which an oppoſition of intereſts, and purſuit of ſeparate views muſt unavoidably produce, if the different preſidencies of India were permitted to act independant of each other, (a fyftem that, however confiftent, or at leaft reconcileable with the inferior interefts of a mere commercial body, could not poffibly be applied to the fituation of the Company as a great political power, which they are at prefent univerfally confidered by the ftates of Hindoftan) the tranfactions of the period I am now relating, fully prove, that even this controling power is at prefent of too circumfcribed a nature, and that, in order to give vigour and ftability to the Britifh empire in India, the firft ftep to which requires a confiftency and uniformity in political meafures, it is abfolutely neceffary, that a full and unlimited authority, in all matters relative to peace or war, and in every negociation with foreign ftates, be delegated to the Governor General and Council, and that the prefidencies of Madras and Bombay be directed, not only to give implicit and unconditional obedience to their orders, but to confider themfelves as immediately and folely refponfible to the Council General for their conduct in the execution of them.

If this plan had been originally adopted, we fhould not afterwards have had to contend with the two moft powerful ftates in India, the Mharattas and Hyder Ally, united with the combined ftrength of France and Holland; nor fhould we be now fuing for peace at the feet of a vanquifhed enemy, who is reaping the harveft of wars he does not fight, and recovering in the Carnatic the territories he has, to every effort of his own force, irrecoverably loft in the Guzerat and Concan.

It is true, the three prefidencies feem in one point to have been moft cordial and unanimous, I mean in their refolution to make war; but although perfectly agreeing in the fame general fyftem, they unfortunately ly differed materially in the particular object to which it should be directed.

In Bengal and in Bombay they mutually marked the Mharattas as the victims of their sanguinary vengeance, but they attempted their destruction by means totally dissimilar and irreconcileable; and whilst the one party was actually in arms, struggling to exalt Ragonaut Row upon the ruins of his country, the other was equally active in opposing a rival to his greatness in the person of the Berar prince.

In Madras, a conduct still more extraordinary and impolitic was adopted, and the business of the Guntoor Sarcar will be a lasting monument of the folly and bad faith of the nation, as well as a reproach to the persons who transacted it. In short, the records of that government, during the period of which I am now treating, exhibit scenes of a treacherous policy, weakness and corruption, which are not to be equalled in the annals of almost any age or country. It would be an endless task, and exceed the intended bounds of this narrative, to enter into a minute description of each particular transaction. — Suffice it to touch upon the subject generally.

Notwithstanding the war then existing with the French and Mharattas, and a knowledge of the resentment already harboured by Hyder Ally against the English, the consequence of which was ever to be apprehended from the rooted rancour and animosity which Mahomed Ally and that chief mutually entertained, the government of Madras, so far from endeavouring to ward off the approaching evil by any temporising or moderate conduct, at once took a step that not only irritated and offended Hyder beyond any hope of reconciliation, but threatened in its consequences to draw on the refentment of Nizam Ally, Soubah of the Decan; nor could a rupture with the latter have been avoided, but by the wife and well-timed interpofition of the Governor General and Council, who cancelled the engagements made with Bazalut Jung, contrary to the faith of treaties then fubfifting betwixt the Englifh and the Nizam, reftored the Guntoor Sarcar, and by farther political advances and feafonable conceffions, feconded by the ability and addrefs of Mr. Holland, who was employed to negociate at the court of Hyderabad, preferved the Nizam in his neutrality, and prevented him from giving any fupport to the Mharatta adminiftration, with whom he was, and ftill continues to be, very clofely connected.

To aggravate Hyder's feelings by every poffible means, in addition to the feizure of the Guntoor Sarcar, and the detaching a force towards Adoni, Bazalut Jung's capital, to defend him againft the refentment of his brother the Nizam and Hyder Ally, that force was directed to march through the territory of the latter, although by a fmall circuit, his country might have been entirely avoided.

This infult, added to former caufes of provocation, and the engagements he had lately formed with the Mharatta minifter, precipitated Hyder's hoftile preparations, and in the middle of the year 1780 he defcended the paffes and entered the Carnatic, which, according to expectation, he found totally unprepared for defence, and unable to oppofe or check his career.

The rapidity of his conquefts and the fatal difafter which befel our arms near Conjeveram, are facts too well known, and too remarkable in their nature, to admit of being mentioned in this place, or even to require any comment. I fhall, therefore, clofe this digreffion gression by the following general reflection; that as the misconduct and imbecility of the Madras government was the cause of Hyder's immediately overrunning and destroying the Carnatic, and possessing himself of many of the principal fortresses almost without opposition, it is also to the operation of that original neglect, which rendered the country an intire desart, that we must ascribe both the subsequent failure of the efforts of the Governor General and Council, who strained every resource to relieve the distress of the Carnatic, and the insufficiency of Sir Eyre Coote's personal exertions, who has, however, acquired immortal glory, for having so long stemmed a torrent he was prevented from making effectual head against; and it is ultimately in the effects of this neglect, we must look for the embarrassment in which even our successes against the Mharattas have involved us, and the disappointment our hopes from them are likely to experience.

I have thus in some degree explained the causes as well as immediate consequences of the war with Hyder, and it now remains to describe the manner in which that event operated upon our contest with the Mharattas.

The first idea which naturally suggested itself to the Governor General and Council, after sending a supply of men and treasure to the coast, was to endeavour to terminate the Mharatta war, in order to employ their whole collected force in opposing Hyder, and driving him from the Carnatic. For this purpose proposals for an accommodation were transmitted to the Poonah administration, and copies of them separately forwarded to the President and Select Committee of Bombay and General Goddard, for their information and observation. The letter to the latter, dated October 9, 1780,

1780, concludes with the following paragraph: " And
" we hereby pofitively require and command you im-
" mediately to fufpend all hoftilities and military ope-
" rations againft the Mharattas, whenever you may
" receive a requifition in writing to that effect from
" the Peifhwa, that the like order had been given on
" his part to the officer commanding his armies; but
" in the mean time, and until fuch requifition and no-
" tification be received by you, we direct that you pro-
" fecute the war with the utmoft vigour, and act in all
" circumftances as if the foregoing information had
" not been fent you."

In the treaty tranfmitted, we offered to relinquifh every conqueft excepting Ahmedabad and Gualior, which had been guarantied to Futty Sing, and the Ranna of Gohud, upon conditions of the Mharattas uniting with us in an offenfive alliance againft Hyder Ally, of whofe dominions a conqueft and mutual divifion was to be made. Should the Mharattas not accede to an offenfive alliance, peace was neverthelefs propofed, each party retaining what it had acquired, or a fufpenfion of hoftilities was to take place on both fides for one year from the date of the treaty, for the purpofe of negociating the terms of a future and perpetual adjuftment. Some ftipulations fufficiently favourable were propofed refpecting Ragonaut Row, and Modajee Bofla's offer of mediation and guarantee on this occafion was declared to be accepted, himfelf permitted to become a party, and the treaty in confequence tranfmitted through him to the minifter at the Mharatta court.

Three months having elapfed from the date of the treaty, and no notification received from the Peifhwa, either of its arrival, or of any refolution he had come

to

to in confequence, the military operations continued to be vigoroufly pufhed, and in the middle of January, 1781, the whole of the army affembled at Vifrabuy, a place about twenty miles inland from Baffein, of remarkable fanctity and religious repute amongft the Hindoos, and where there are fome hot wells, deemed of great medicinal efficacy.

A part of the army had been encamped in its neighbourhood ever fince the 14th of the preceding month, at which time General Goddard arrived himfelf with the grenadiers from before Baffein, to the feafonable relief of a detachment of Bombay troops, which had been employed for a confiderable period before in the fouthern parts of the Concan, protecting the country and collecting the grain. The harveft was then over, and the troops on their march towards Baffein had advanced as far as the neighbourhood of Vifrabuy, where, having fuccefsfully oppofed fmaller parties of the enemy, they were at length attacked and furrounded by fuperior force, and compelled to take poft in a very ftrong and advantageous fituation, from which it would have been equally difficult for the enemy to diflodge them, as it was impoffible for them to advance. This force, at the time of which I am now fpeaking, acted under the feparate and particular orders of the Select Committee at Bombay, but was afterwards put under General Goddard's fole command, and continued fo the remainder of the campaign.

The Concan is a tract of country extending confiderably along the fea coaft, and is feparated from the Decan on the eaftward by a chain * of high hills, running

in

---

* This chain extends itfelf all along the Malabar coaft, almoft as far to the fouthward as Anjengo; and the entrance into

the

in a direction from north to south, and parallel with the shore, over which, in such places as are most acceſſible, the several gauts or paſſes leading into the Mharatta country, which from its great elevation is ſtiled the Balagaut, are ſituated.

At the time the army marched from Baſſein, the force of the Mharattas in the Concan and below the gauts, under Hurry Punt Furkea, conſiſted of at leaſt twenty thouſand horſe and foot, with about fifteen guns. Theſe were poſted on the road to Bhore Gaut, which is one of the moſt eaſy and practicable paſſes, and where it was expected by the enemy we meant to aſcend, being the neareſt and moſt convenient route to Poonah, and having been preferred by the Bombay government on a former occaſion.

Notwithſtanding their numbers, they were too much intimidated to offer any ſerious oppoſition, and excepting a few ſlight ſkirmiſhes, in which we were always ſuperior, the army met with little or no reſiſtance till it reached Campoley, at the entrance of the Bhore Gaut, on the 8th of February. The enemy had previouſly aſcended, and from appearances there was every reaſon to believe they had come to a determination of reſolutely diſputing the paſſage. This belief was confirmed by the ſpies, who gave intelligence, that about four thouſand infantry with guns had taken poſt

---

the Myſore country, and the whole of Hyder's dominions on the weſtern ſide of India, is in like manner rendered difficult and hazardous by ſteep and narrow paſſes over them, which muſt neceſſarily require any plan of military operations entered into from that quarter to be formed upon a very liberal and therefore expenſive ſcale, not only to anſwer any real and adequate purpoſe of public advantage, but to guard againſt the danger of miſcarriage, to which it would be otherwiſe certainly expoſed.

upon

upon the top of it, that the whole Mharatta army was encamped at a little diſtance, and that Holkar, with about fifteen thouſand men from Malwa, and another chief, called Ragonaut Pundit, with about half that number, had lately arrived in their camp.

The General confidering that any delay would not only encreaſe the confidence of the enemy, but give them an opportunity of conſtructing new works, ſo as to render the paſs every day more difficult and hazardous, reſolved upon ſtorming it that very night. The grenadiers were accordingly ordered to be in readineſs, under the command of Colonel Parker, and a plan of attack formed, which from its own judicioufneſs and excellence, the gallantry and good conduct of the officer who executed it, and the diſciplined, ſteady valour of the troops under him, proved ſuccefsful beyond even the moſt ſanguine expectation. The party entered the foot of the paſs at midnight, and by five in the morning had gained entire poſſeſſion of it, driving the enemy from Condolah, the very ſummit of the hill, and four miles diſtant from Campoley, moſt of the road winding through narrow defiles, and up a very ſteep and rugged aſcent.

Poonah, the Mharatta capital, is not diſtant from Bhore Gaut more than forty-five miles. Such were the terrors impreſſed upon the enemy, in confequence of our near approach, and ſo ſtrong their belief of our intentions to advance towards it, that they entirely burnt and deſtroyed Telliagong, a very confiderable town about half way, and had actually made every preparation for ſetting fire to Poonah itſelf, by filling the houſes with ſtraw, and removing the inhabitants and effects to the neighbourhood of Settara.

K A know-

A knowledge of this circumstance united with many other considerations to prevent our pushing forward to the capital, and to confine the remaining operations of the campaign to a defence of the conquests already made.

In the first place, our whole force did not exceed six thousand men, and the enemy's could not be less than eight times that number; it was therefore impossible to make any division of our force, or even to leave a detachment sufficiently strong to defend the post at Bhore Gaut if we advanced beyond it. Unassisted by horse, we could entertain but little hope of being able to collect provision or even procure forage in a country totally desolate and ruined, and we must on that account have carried a very ample supply of grain with us, which would of course have greatly encumbered and endangered our march.

In addition to these considerations, when we reflect that no adequate or useful end could possibly be attained by entering the Decan, either towards improving the success of the war, or bringing it to a termination, that we had not the most distant expectation of being joined by any party in the Mharatta state, which alone would have justified our advancing; and that without any determinate object to gratify, or hope of a revolution to excite us, we could only have acquired the empty glory of possessing the Mharatta capital for a few days, and of effecting a retreat from it at the most eminent peril and certain hazard: I say, when these matters come to be fully considered, the impropriety and impolicy of penetrating into the Decan, under such an accumulation of discouraging circumstances, will be clear and obvious to every one.

The rapid progress of our arms had hitherto produced no overture or notification on the part of the Peishwa, according to the expectations derived from the contents of the Bengal letter; on the contrary, it appeared that the minister, from the time of receiving the Bengal proposals, had become more remiss and indifferent in his endeavours to accomplish a peace, which from our extreme anxiety and solicitude, he saw it was in his power to obtain whenever it might suit his own inclination or convenience, upon terms far superiour to his most sanguine expectations.

The near approach of the army seemed, however, to rouse him from this security; and a few days after getting possession of the gauts, a message arrived from one Byroo Pundit, proposing to send an emissary to the camp, to converse upon the subject of negociation.

This Byroo Pundit possessed a considerable share of the private confidence of the minister, and had entered into a secret correspondence with General Goddard so early as the month of October 1780, to which the latter gave every proper encouragement, in order to avail himself of any means it might offer for accomplishing a peace. Nana Furnese was himself privy to the whole transaction; and this renewal of correspondence, after it had been suspended for above two months, induced the General to form some hopes favourable to peace. He therefore determined to promote it all in his power, and answered Byroo Pundit's letter, by consenting to his proposal of sending an emissary, who accordingly arrived in camp the 12th of February.

All expectations of success, however, from this circumstance soon vanished; and the man, after affirming that " although the minister wished to unite with the " English against Hyder Ally hereafter, it was his pre-
" sent

" fent determination to adhere to the engagements he
" had made with that chief, and to make no treaty
" with the Englifh in which he was not included," returned to his mafter, promifing to communicate faithfully the friendly intentions of the Englifh, and the particular points given to him in charge by the General; in confequence of which, fhould the minifter approve, a public vakeel from the Sarcar fhould be immediately deputed to negociate, or at all events an anfwer fhould be returned in eight days. The anfwer was written by Byroo Pundit, and repeated the minifter's determination, " to make no treaty with the Englifh
" in which Hyder Ally was not included as a friend
" and ally of the Peifhwa."

As Byroo Pundit s agent had declared in converfation, that the propofals for peace from Bengal had never been received by the minifter, the General thought it proper, that he might not have it in his power hereafter to plead ignorance of them, as an excufe for continuing the war, and to obtain a decided knowledge of his prefent intentions, to fend him a copy of the propofals, declaring himfelf empowered to conclude an alliance with the Mharattas, and ready to accede to one upon the terms offered by the Governor General and Council.

The minifter's anfwer, as it was clear and pointed with refpect to his own intentions, and furnifhed an additional proof of the fincere and friendly inclinations of the Berar prince, I fhall here tranfcribe. —
" Before this time, Modajee Bofla wrote to the Sarcar
" as follows: The Governor General and Council of
" Calcutta have fent a treaty to me, but as it does not
" meet with my approbation, how can it be approved
" and conceded to by the Peifhwa ? — I have therefore
returned

"returned it to Mr. Haſtings." The miniſter proceeds — "At preſent that very treaty which you have "ſent me has been peruſed by your friend from begin- "ning to end, and it is certain that the contents there- "in written are not proper or fit for the approbation "of the Sarcar. If you are ſincere and fervent in "your deſire of friendſhip, it is incumbent upon you "to make a treaty that ſhall include the propoſals of "thoſe who are allied to, and connected with the "counſels of the Sarcar."

Thus ended all attempts to negociate during this campaign, the particulars of which were faithfully and minutely communicated to the Government of Bengal, as well as to the Select Committee of Bombay, with whoſe immediate advice and concurrence they had been conducted.

The remaining military operations were reſtricted entirely to a plan of defence; and excepting ſome ſmart, though partial attacks, made by very conſiderable bodies of the enemy, upon the eſcorts of proviſions coming to the army from Pownwell, in which Colonel George Brown and Major Donald Mackay, of the Madras eſtabliſhment, who commanded on two ſeparate occaſions, acquired great honour and credit, the Mharattas contented themſelves with now and then advancing towards the poſt at Condolah, on the top of the gauts, with an appearance of reſolution and vigour, which, however, was ſure to fail them whenever any correſponding movements were made on our ſide, or after diſcharging a few effectual ſhot amongſt them.

In repeated letters from Sir Eyre Coote, who was at that time preparing for the important conteſt with Hyder Ally in the Carnatic, the moſt earneſt and preſſing recommendations had been uſed for making a powerful diverſion

diverſion in favour of his operations, by an attack upon Hyder's dominions from the Malabar coaſt.

The continuation of the Mharatta war, and the poſitive refuſal of the miniſter to accede to an alliance, unfortunately rendered ſuch a meaſure abſolutely impracticable. The utmoſt exertion that could poſſibly be made on the weſtern ſide of India, while engaged in a conteſt with the whole Mharatta empire, was to relieve the Madras troops at Tellicherry * by an equal proportion from Bombay, and to ſend the former round to the coaſt of Coromandel.

In order to effect this as early as poſſible, General Goddard found it neceſſary to deſcend the gauts, and to march towards the ſea coaſt. He accordingly concerted his operations with ſuch ſkill and ſecreſy, that the whole of the artillery and heavy ſtores reached the foot of the paſs in ſafety, and without the ſmalleſt interruption from the enemy, who, indeed, remained unapprized of his intentions, and were aſtoniſhed in the morning of the 18th of April, to find that the poſt had been deſerted during the preceding night.

The country through which the route of the army lay to the ſea coaſt, was of a nature remarkably well calculated to reſiſt any impreſſion from large bodies of horſe, being exceedingly full of thick buſhes and jungles, broken ground and narrow defiles, where it would be impoſſible, except in very few places, for cavalry to act together. It was not, however, the leſs dangerous

---

* This is a valuable ſettlement upon the coaſt of Malabar, dependant upon the preſidency of Bombay, which the Madras detachment had garriſoned, after the capture of Mahé from the French, and had defended it againſt the attacks of the Nairs, tributary to Hyder Ally.

to the march of our troops, who had a perfect contempt for the moft impetuous charge of the moft numerous army of Mharatta horfe, and could only be effentially injured by parties of infantry concealed in hollow ways and behind rocks and bufhes, for which the fituation of the country proved peculiarly favourable.

This mode of attack was accordingly adopted by the enemy, who defcended into the Concan, under Hurry Punt Furkea, Tuckojee Holkar, and Purrifs Ram Bow, three of their principal chiefs. Their number could not be fhort of fifty thoufand men, of which near ten thoufand were infantry, moft of them Arabs and Sindys, who, excepting the fepoys regularly trained up in the European difcipline, are by far the braveft and moft ferviceable troops in Hindoftan.

The diftance from the foot of the gauts to the fea was about twenty-four miles, and during the whole of the march, which lafted three days, the enemy exerted their utmoft efforts to harrafs and annoy the line, but without producing any other effect than unfortunately killing and wounding fome of our people. They fuffered very confiderably themfelves, but were unable to obtain the fmalleft partial advantage over the Englifh troops, or even to feize upon any part of the great quantity of neceffary baggage and ftores which attended them: a circumftance that reflects the higheft honour upon the military conduct and fkilful manœuvres of the commander, and upon the fteady valour and gallant perfeverance of the whole army.

This fevere action of three days continuance, in which Colonel Parker, the fecond in command, gallantly loft his life, and which has been fucceeded by no farther military efforts of any confequence, either on our part or that of the Mharattas, terminated the
opera-

operations of the fecond campaign, as the enemy fhortly after afcending the gauts, evacuated the Concan, and the Englifh army prepared to canton at Callián during the approaching winter.

That I might not interrupt my narrative of the tranfactions on the Malabar coaft, I have not regarded the precife order of time, in communicating what was performed during this campaign on the fide of Malawa.

In the beginning of the feafon, purfuant to the plan before propofed, and which had been moft ftrongly recommended by General Goddard, in order to employ Scindia and Holkar at a diftance from the fcene of his operations, it had been refolved to augment the force in that quarter; and notwithftanding the preferable claims of Major Popham, from his having already diftinguifhed himfelf in the command, he was unjuftly deprived of it, and the conduct of the operations on their propofed extenfive plan committed to another officer, whofe merits, however great they might otherwife be, ought not to have been put in competition with Major Popham's fuperior pretenfions on this particular occafion.

Another and more capital error, becaufe attended with injury to the public, was the infufficiency of the exertions themfelves, and the inferiority of the force employed, even after the propofed augmentation had taken place, to anfwer any important purpofe of real or adequate benefit; by which means it happened, that Scindia, confidering himfelf as fully equal to oppofe its progrefs, detached Holkar with a confiderable body of troops to fupport the minifter; and notwithwithftanding the decreafe of oppofition, the detachment itfelf, after advancing as far as Seronge, which is near one hundred miles north of the Nerbuddah, found

it

it neceffary to retreat towards the country of the Ranna of Gohud; in effecting which, Colonel Camac, who commanded, planned, and executed with fuccefs a judicious march upon Scindia, furprifing his camp, and taking fome guns and elephants, and by that means profecuted the remainder of his march to the northward with lefs moleftation and difficulty.

I have thus conducted my narrative to the conclufion of the fecond campaign of the Mharatta war; and here it may be proper to paufe, in order to take a furvey of the general ftate of affairs at that period, as an attention to, and knowledge of them, is abfolutely neceffary to form a proper judgment of the meafures afterwards adopted.

In addition to the conquefts of the preceding year, Baffein and the country of the Concan, extending along the fea coaft from Bombay to Surat, had been acquired for the Company, which completed every view of territorial poffeffion their moft fanguine wifhes, encouraged by the moft fignal and glorious fucceffes, could have ever led them to expect, or even hope for. To balance thefe advantages, Hyder Ally had invaded and overrun the Carnatic, where he feemed to have eftablifhed himfelf fo firmly, by poffeffing many of the ftrong holds, and laying wafte the whole of the open country, that any adequate exertion from that quarter to drive him out of it was judged abfolutely beyond our ftrength and impracticable. It became, therefore, the chief and primary object of our political confideration, to attack Hyder's dominions from the coaft of Malabar; nor is there any doubt but that this expedient, could it have been vigoroufly and extenfively adopted, muft have fully anfwered every propofed ufeful end, and have delivered the Carnatic from its dangerous,

gerous, its fatal invader. In effecting this point, however, the difficulty lay, for it was obvious to the plainest sense and most common understanding, that some accommodation with the Mharatta state was a necessary prelude to any attack on Hyder from Bombay. Accordingly proposals had been transmitted for that purpose to Poonah, through the Rajah of Berar, as has been already seen; and although the enmity naturally subsisting between the Peishwa and Hyder Ally, and the advantage taken by the latter during the late troubles in the Mharatta government, of possessing himself of an immense territory south of the river Kristna, yielding annually near a crore of rupees, might have encouraged a reasonable hope of the minister's eagerly embracing an opportunity to recover such valuable possessions, it was unfortunately found, that a resentment of our conduct, a sense of obligation to Hyder for his seasonable interposition, and a confidence in the important benefits expected from their mutual connection, prevailed over every other consideration, and determined him to prefer his late engagements to an advantageous alliance with the English, even though it came recommended to his acceptance by an immediate restitution of all the conquests we had made since the commencement of the war.

This determination on the part of the minister to persevere in hostilities, rendered any invasion of Hyder's territories from the Malabar coast utterly impossible, and while it pointed out the necessity of previously bringing the Mharatta contest to a determination, suggested a vigorous prosecution of hostilities, as the only effectual and speedy means of doing so.

That these were the sentiments of the Government of Bengal, will appear from the following extract of
their

their letter to the Select Committee of Bombay, dated May 10, 1781. " We have repeatedly declared, that " we wish sincerely a peace with the Mharatta state. " It is our fixed object, and we shall deem the accom- " plishment of it on honourable terms a most desirable " event. One mode of obtaining it has been tried, " advances have been made, but these advances have " not been successful. A repetition of them would in " our opinion have no other effect, than to fix an opi- " nion of our weakness in the Mharatta government, " and instead of shortening, prolong the duration of " the war.*

" We repeat our firm conviction, that nothing but " a vigorous and successful prosecution of it, will pro- " duce an honourable termination to it. Under this im- " pression, our instructions to General Goddard have " been framed and continued; and under the same in- " fluence we express to you our wish, that your aid " may be afforded to General Goddard's operation."

Notwithstanding this decided opinion of the Governor General and Council, for a vigorous prosecution of the war against the Mharattas, the most urgent and pointed representations of the necessity of making a powerful diversion on the side of Malabar, were constantly arriving from the coast of Coromandel; and the consequences of neglecting to do so immediately, were displayed in the most lively and alarming colours, without any reference to the actual state of circumstances at Bombay, or to the certain ruin with which

* How sincerely is it to be lamented, that this obvious and self-evident maxim did not always strike the Governor General and Council in the same forcible and convincing manner, as it seems to have done on the present occasion.

that prefidency would be menaced from the Mharattas, if the force neceffary for its protection and fecurity was detached upon any remote or feparate fervice.

In this exigency, the government of Bombay, in concert with General Goddard, ftrained every nerve they poffibly could without leaving themfelves entirely defencelefs; and they certainly had merit in the difintereftednefs with which they were willing to relinquifh the rich prize within their grafp, and to facrifice every hope of their own future aggrandizement, to their defire of contributing to the immediate relief of the diftrefs of the Carnatic. With this view, they fent the greateft part of the Madras detachment round to the Coromandel coaft, immediately after the return of the army from the gouts, although from every argument of a juft and rational policy, confirmed by the declared opinion of the Governor General and Council, it was fuppofed that the fucceeding campaign muft be entered upon with energy and vigour, in order to extricate the Company's affairs from the misfortunes that generally threatened their deftruction; and in the fubfequent November, when it was found their own hands were effectually tied up from active operations, as will appear in the fequel, they fent down an additional reinforcement to the garrifon of Tellichery, which enabled Major Abingdon, the officer commanding, to make a gallant, fudden, and well-concerted fally from the place, furprize the camp, totally defeat and difperfe the army of the Befiegers, and take Sardar Chawn, Hyder Ally's general, prifoner, who died fhortly after of his wounds. This fuccefs was vigoroufly purfued by Major Abingdon, and followed by the capture of Callicut; and although thefe facts happened many months after the period of which I am now treating, I have introduced
them

them here, that they may not interrupt the detail of more important tranfactions.

Before I enter upon the latter, I think it alfo neceffary to mention a circumftance relative to General Goddard, whofe appointment * of commander in chief

at

* I have been the more particular on this fubject, becaufe from the manner in which the command of the Bengal troops was continued to General Goddard by the Court of Directors, he certainly was entitled to retain it during their ftay on the Malabar coaft; and his accepting the ftation of commander in chief at Bombay, was in compliance with the wifhes of the Company, and in obedience to their orders, nor could it in any fhape deftroy his unalienable right to the command of the Bengal detachment. In order to prove this, I fhall tranfcribe the orders of the Company, appointing General Goddard, dated April 12, 1780.

Paragraph 21. Having taken into our particular and moft ferious confideration, the ftate of the Company's military force at your fettlement, we have refolved to appoint an able officer to the command of the troops at Bombay.

Par. 22. And having the higheft opinion of the zeal, experience, and military abilities of Colonel Thomas Goddard, we have thought fit to appoint Colonel Goddard commander in chief of the Company's forces at Bombay, and granted him a commiffion of brigadier general in our fervice.

Par. 27. It is our order, that Brigadier-general Goddard have a conftant feat as third in our faid Council and Select Committee.

Par. 28. And as a farther mark of our approbation of the conduct of Brigadier-general Goddard, we have directed, that the pay and allowances received by him from Bengal, as commander in chief of the detachment fent from that fettlement, be continued to him, and paid by our Governor General and Council, fo long as thofe troops fhall remain under General Goddard's command on the weftern fide of India. He muft receive the pay

and

at Bombay had been received there in October, 1780, but from the important services on which he had ever since been employed, and his absence from the presidency, he had not entered upon the immediate and particular discharge of that trust until the month of June, 1781, when he received a letter from the Governor and Council of Bombay on the subject, an extract of which I shall here transcribe. " The Select " Committee have acquainted us, that soon after the " receipt of the Company's orders of the 12th of " April, 1780, they have transmitted to you a copy " of such parts as related to yourself; in answer to " which you informed them, that you had forwarded " a copy thereof to the Governor General and Coun- " cil, and waited their sentiments thereon. As a con- " siderable time has since elapsed, and you are now " come to reside here during the monsoon, we request " to know whether it is the intention of the Bengal " government and your own wish to accept of the sta- " tion and appointments which the honourable Com- " pany have conferred on you."

His reply, chearfully agreeing to enter upon the immediate discharge of the duties of the chief command, was conveyed in the following very clear and unambiguous terms. " I beg leave, in answer to your requi- " sition upon the subject of the orders of the honour-

and allowance of third of our Council and Select Committee at Bombay ; but if our Governor General and Council shall recall the Bengal detachment, the pay and allowances received by General Goddard on that account, must be discontinued and cease immediately upon the return of the said detachment, as it will be then no longer under his authority or command; and after that period, General Goddard must receive the pay and allowances of our commander in chief of our troops at Bombay.

" able

"able Court of Directors of the 12th of April, to
"transmit a paragraph of a letter received from the
"honourable Governor General and Council, which is
"as follows: 'We have great pleasure in congratu-
'lating you on the marks of distinction conferred on
'you by the honourable the Court of Directors, in
'their orders of the 12th of April, as honourable in
'themselves, as they have been deservedly bestowed,
'in reward and approbation of your services and con-
'duct.'

"Although the above answer contains no positive
"declaration of the wishes of the honourable Gover-
"nor General and Council, yet I consider it as tacitly
"implying an approbation of, and sanction to, my ac-
"ceptance of the important charge which our ho-
"nourable masters have been pleased to honour me
"with; and therefore beg leave to acquaint you, that
"as it appears to me to coincide with the intention of
"the Bengal government, so it is my own wish to ac-
"cept of the station and appointments conferred on
"me by the honourable Company, and I am ready to
"enter upon the discharge of the duties they impose,
"whenever this government shall deem my services
"requisite.

"I think it proper in this place to mention, that by
"so doing I by no means intend, nor is it at all a ne-
"cessary consequence I should, to depart from the line
"prescribed for my guidance by the honourable Go-
"vernor General and Council, in the general conduct
"of the Mharatta war, and that in all matters rela-
"tive to it, as well as what regards the Bengal de-
"tachment under my command, I must consider my-
"self as subject to the exclusive and particular orders
"of

"of that presidency, in any manner they may think
"expedient and necessary for the service."

I shall now resume my narrative, which is, indeed, drawing to a conclusion; and it is a painful reflection, that the few facts remaining to be told, will unfortunately discover the same want of decision and vigour in the councils, and of prudence and firmness in the measures of the Bengal government, which have so conspicuously marked the whole of their political transactions with the Mharatta state, without the pleasing detail of conquest and military success that has hitherto diversified and enlivened the subject.

Impressed with the firm conviction of the necessity of terminating the Mharatta war, previous to the possibility of undertaking any important or adequate enterprize against Hyder from the coast of Malabar, and assured from past experience of the determined spirit of the Poonah Durbar, that an object so desirable could only be attained by a vigorous and successful prosecution of hostilities, General Goddard, as early as the month of July, 1781, prepared a plan of operations for the ensuing campaign, and laid it before the Select Committee of Bombay, who concurred in its expediency, and immediately transmitted it to the government of Bengal for their approbation and assistance to carry it into effectual execution.

In the mean time every necessary and leading step was taken on the part of the Bombay government and General Goddard which depended upon, or could be effected by, their own means; and the latter, notwithstanding the severe and tempestuous weather which renders the navigation on the Malabar coast extremely hazardous, and almost impracticable during the months of June, July, and August, sailed for Surat, at which
place

place he arrived the 2d of the latter month. He shortly after effected an interview with Futty Sing, and obtained from that chief a body of five thousand horse for the service of the ensuing campaign, which was two thousand more than the number he was bound to furnish by treaty.

This important point being accomplished, and a proper provision and disposition of the force in Guzerat, both for the defence of that province, and for co-operating with the detachment * stationed on the northern confines of Malwa, whose active services and future junction constituted a necessary part of the intended plan, the General returned to Bombay; and after the vigorous exertions he had made, and the sanguine expectations he had been led to form of success, it is easy to conceive how great must have been his mortification and disappointment to find that the only benefit to be hoped for from all his zealous endeavours, was the alarm which it could not fail to excite in the mind of the Mharatta minister, and that he must be compelled to restrict his own future operations to a system of mere defence.

But before I explain the causes of this disappointment, it is proper to take notice of some events which happened in Bengal during the monsoon. On the 11th of June, the Governor General and Council renewed the credentials they had before given to General God-

---

* After its return to the northward, the command devolved upon Colonel Muir, who in consequence of Colonel Camac's letters from Seronge, had been detached across the Jumna to his assistance, and had advanced as far as the Rana of Gohud's country, before the news of Colonel Camac's successful retreat reached him.

dard, impowering him to conclude a treaty with the Mharatta ſtate, either in caſe of receiving overtures to that end directly from the Poonah government, or in caſe of the arrival of Dewaghur Pundit,* Modajee Boſla's Dewan at Poonah, for the purpoſe of mediating a peace betwixt the Engliſh and Mharatta powers.

In the inſtructions furniſhed at this time, after declaring the treaty tendered to the Mharatta government in the preceding October, to be the baſis of that propoſed to be now concluded, they particularly except the ceſſion of the fort and territory of Baſſein, which they ſay, as the miniſter did not chooſe to avail himſelf of their former proffer, and conſidering the very favourable turn which their affairs have ſince taken, they are of opinion that they are warranted in reſerving, if they can, for the benefit of the Company.

In a ſubſequent paragraph of the ſame letter, they recede from the above determination in the following words: " If the miniſter ſhall refuſe to yield up the

---

* Here we unfortunately ſee the unaccountable predilection in favour of Modajee, the Rajah of Berar, and ill-placed confidence in his friendſhip, operating with an equal degree of force to what it had done upon ſo many preceding occaſions, notwithſtanding the leſſons we might have learnt from his conduct when General Goddard's detachment arrived on the confines of his country, on its march to Bombay; from his acceding to the general confederacy in the middle of 1779, and afterwards detaching a body of troops, under his ſon Chimnajee, towards Bengal; from the too ſucceſsful arts he had practiſed, to retard and obſtruct the early advance of Colonel Camac's detachment to regain Scindia's capital; and from the line of treacherous policy he adopted much about the ſame time, with reſpect to the propoſals for peace with the Poonah government, tranſmitted through him in October 1780.

" pre-

"pretensions of the Peishwa to Bassein, and to accede
"to a treaty either of alliance or peace unless it be re-
"stored, we empower you in such case to give it up.
"This is a point of which, having expressed our wishes
"as far as we can propose them for effect, we must
"finally and wholly rely on your discretion, to decide
"it in whatever manner you shall judge best for attain-
"ing the sole end which we have in view, which is
"Peace. In all events, an honourable and equal peace,
"and if it can be attained, an advantageous one."

I have been the more particular in transcribing the above paragraph, because it proves, that the Governor General and Council, at the time of penning these instructions, had not adopted those desponding and melancholy sentiments which have since prostrated them at the feet of an insulting, though vanquished enemy; and that General Goddard's opinion, repeatedly urged both to the Government of Bengal and to the Select Committee of Bombay, "that no peace could be ob-
"tained with the Mharattas but by a vigorous and
"successful prosecution of hostilities, and that solici-
"tude and anxiety on our part would only tend to en-
"crease the confidence of the minister, and the inso-
"lent extravagance of his demands," was, at the period I am now speaking of, countenanced by the declared ideas of the Governor General and Council themselves.

Their letters concluded with acquainting General Goddard, that it being the Governor General's intention to proceed to Lucknow about the middle of July, he would of course take Benares on his way, and probably Modajee's Dewan might lay aside his first design of a journey to Poonah, and give the Governor General a meeting at Benares,* in which cafe, he, the General, was to continue his negociation with the Mharatta government, but fufpend the execution of the treaty, and conftantly advife the Governor General of his proceedings, and of every thing material to be known.

Whatever effect might be produced from the intended vifit of Modajee's Dewan to Poonah, it feemed to the General pretty certain, that no overture could reafonably be expected directly from the Poonah government, and that they would continue to be directed by the fame policy as the preceding year, wifely avoiding any advances themfelves, fince they had it in their power to conclude a treaty whenever they might find it convenient, upon fuch conditions as they fhould judge moft for their intereft, and confiftent with the actual ftate of circumftances at the time.

It was for this powerful reafon, and becaufe no adequate or ferious attack could poffibly be made upon Hyder's dominions from the coaft of Malabar, until fome previous fettlement either of peace or alliance fhould take place with the Mharattas, that the Bombay government and General Goddard were defirous of adopting vigorous meafures,† and of making one great and formidable exertion of all the force which they could

---

* It unfortunately happened that Dewaghur Pundit, Modajee's Dewan, fell fick about this time, and died fhortly after, fo that his intended journey either to Poonah or Benares never took place, and the fincerity of Modajee's friendfhip luckily efcaped the very fevere and arduous trial it muft otherwife have undergone.

† It appears by a minute of General Goddard's, at the Select Committee of Bombay, early in November, that this opinion of the

could themselves collect, generally aided by the Governor General and Council, and particularly supported by the operations of their detachment under Colonel Muir, in order to imprefs the Poonah minifter with that belief of our yet unreduced ftrength, and apprehenfion of his own future lofs and danger, which they were juftly fenfible could alone produce a difpofition favourable to our views of peace, or even procure a timely fufpenfion of hoftilities; nor was it till the month of November, 1781, that they found themfelves compelled to abandon every idea of acting offenfively, and to accommodate themfelves as far as the neceffary attention to their own fafety would permit, to the new fyftem adopted in Bengal, and the meafures lately purfued in confequence of it. I have already hinted Mr. Haftings's intention of proceeding to Lucknow. He accordingly left Calcutta, and arrived at Benares the middle of Auguft, in the neighbourhood of which his journey terminated, for he was compelled to retire into the fortrefs of Chunar, as an afylum from the hoftile vengeance and fpirited refentment of Rajah Cheyt Sing, a Zemindar, who rented the rich city and

---

the neceffity of preferving an appearance of vigour was ftrongly fupported by the contents of a letter from Mr. Holland, refident at the court of Hydexabad, dated Sept. 2, 1781, where, after acquainting the General that he had a negociation on foot with the Nizam for an alliance againft Hyder Ally, he fays, " I don't " know what your plan of operations may be; if the cypher " reaches you fafe, I fhould be obliged to you for information, " as they may very materially concern my movements in the ne-" gociation. If an active campaign be not intended, yet the " giving out a report of fuch intention, and making fome move-" ments to favour it, the Nizam thinks will be of ufe in difpo-" fing the Mharattas to liften to terms of accommodation."

depen-

dependencies of Benares under the Englifh Company; and to this place Affuph ul Dowla, Nawab of Oude, arrived in perfon to his relief and enlargement; by which means an opportunity offered of fettling the bufinefs which carried the Governor General towards Lucknow, without proceeding any farther.*

It was under the impreffion of the alarm and confufion which the tumult at Benares excited, and I am willing to believe, the difppointments given to his hopes of Dewaghur Pundit's vifiting Poonah or Benares, that Mr. Haftings authorized the officer in command of the northern detachment, to conclude a feparate treaty with Mahadjee Scindia; by which it was ftipulated, that the Englifh troops fhould immediately recrofs the Jumna, and Scindia promifed on his part to endeavour to negociate a treaty of peace betwixt Hyder Ally and the Englifh, and betwixt the Peifhwa and the Englifh; in which fhould he not fucceed, he agreed to remain neuter in our future contefts with them.

Thefe were the only articles of any importance to the general interefts of the Company, and the termination of the Mharatta war. The reft provided for the fecurity of fome of the petty Rajahs who had taken part with us, but in fuch loofe and indefinite terms,

---

* As the particulars are tedious, and unneceffary to a knowledge of the Mharatta affairs, I have thought it moft proper to avoid a detail of Mr. Haftings's tranfactions with the Rajah of Benares, as well as of the bufinefs fettled with the Vizier at this meeting. It is fufficient here to obferve, that the Governor General's object upon the prefent occafion was to raife a fum of money, in which he materially fucceeded, and that the public neceffities had in his opinion fully juftified the following maxim upon political, if not moral principles: " Get money, honeftly if you " can; but at all events get money."

that

that it was plain we had shamefully sacrificed them to our own political views; as the free and unmolested enjoyment of their possessions was secured to them only during their own good behaviour, or, in other words, during the pleasure of Mahadjee Scindia.*

A copy of this treaty was received by General Goddard, at Bombay, in November; and at the same time a letter arrived from the Governor General, explaining his views in making a treaty with Mahadjee Scindia, and his expectations of that chief's mediating a peace betwixt the English and the Mharattas, as well as of a cessation of arms being immediately agreed to for that purpose.

This point, however, Scindia seems to have considered himself as incompetent to settle; and Colonel Muir, in his letter which accompanied the treaty, only says, that he had promised Scindia to recommend a cessation of hostilities should take place as soon as possible. It is worthy of remark also, that Scindia, in the very article which stipulates an endeavour on his part to negociate a peace betwixt the English and Mharattas, agrees to attempt the same good office betwixt the English and Hyder; and his promise to remain neuter if unsuccessful, offers no material advantage to our future ope-

* The fortress of Gualior had been delivered over to the Ranna of Gohud some months previous to the treaty; and it was expressly stipulated with Scindia, that he should continue to possess it, but under the restriction above mentioned: accordingly, Scindia shortly after, no doubt upon the clearest and most convincing proofs of his guilt, commenced hostilities against him, and desolated his country. A useful lesson, amongst many others, to the princes of Hindostan, how far they repose a confidence in English honour and generosity.

operations in the one cafe more than in the other, fince his perfonal attendance might eafily be difpenfed with, and no diminution of the real ftrength and refources of the Mharatta nation take place ; nor could he, as a fubject of the Peifhwa, detain the revenue or military force of the provinces in his own hands, without exceeding a neutral part, and acting in oppofition to the eftablifhed authority of the Poonah minifter, which I am perfuaded, and a furvey of his whole conduct will prove the affertion, it never has been, nor will it in future be, either his intention or his intereft to do.

About the time of this treaty's arrival at Bombay, the Select Committee alfo received a letter from Fort St. George, under the fignature of Lord Macartney, Sir Eyre Coote, Sir Edward Hughes, and Mr. Macpherfon, one of the members of the Supreme Council of Bengal, to which place he was then on his way from Europe, inclofing a copy of one which they had jointly addreffed to the Peifhwa, with offers of peace, in the name of the Company, the King and Parliament of Great Britain, and promifes, that the Governor General and Council would make a treaty upon the conditions wifhed for by the Peifhwa, with which they declared themfelves fully acquainted.

This felf-created dictatorial junto, in their letter to Bombay, ufe the following very extraordinary expreffions : " It is our meaning, that all hoftilities do im-
" mediately ceafe on the part of the government of
" Bombay, in the fame manner as hoftilities ceafe on
" the part of the Mharattas," and conclude by acquainting the committee, that they may expect to receive inftructions from Bengal of a fimilar nature as foon as poffible, and that this letter would be forwarded
to

to them through the channel of the Mharattas, to whom they had tranfmitted it for that purpofe.*

In confequence of the earneft folicitude for peace expreffed in the Madras letter, and the effectual bar which that circumftance, as well as the recall of the Malwa detachment, occafioned to every hope of terminating the Mharatta war, by a vigorous and fuccefsful campaign, General Goddard, in order that he might be immediately enabled to turn the force on the Malabar coaft againft Hyder Ally, and confidering a treaty with the Peifhwa as a neceffary leading ftep, propofed to the Select Committee of Bombay, to make overtures to the Poonah minifter for commencing a negociation. This meafure they highly approved of, and a letter was accordingly difpatched, generally expreffing the friendly difpofition and inclinations of the Englifh, and offering to depute a confidential perfon to the Peifhwa's court.

Although the government of Bombay, as well as General Goddard, could not with propriety indulge the hope of effecting an alliance with the Mharattas, upon

---

* As a proof of the unfavourable effect which thefe earneft folicitations for peace on our part, and urged in fo extraordinary a ftile, certainly produced in the mind of the minifter, it may not be amifs to obferve, that the original of the above letter, though received at Poonah, was never forwarded to Bombay; and that when Captain Watherfton afterwards expreffed his furprife to Nana Furnefe at his neglecting to do fo, he acknowledged in reply, that it appeared to him a matter of too little confequence to deferve any ferious attention. The truth, however, really was, that the eagernefs and anxiety we imprudently difcovered, had fully convinced the minifter of our weaknefs and diftrefs, and that it would always be in his power to chufe the time, as well as dictate the terms of a treaty with the Englifh.

the conditions which the Bengal inftructions to the latter of the 11th of June, 1781, authorifed, they juftly confidered, that fome overture on their part was requifite to convince the minifter, that they pofleffed the fame pacific intentions with the other prefidencies; and they reafonably concluded, that frefh inftructions, fubfequent to the agreement with Scindia, and to the difpatch of the Fort St. George letter, would have been tranfmitted to General Goddard, at that time publicly invefted with plenipotentiary powers from Bengal at the Mharatta court, and in all probability arrive at Bombay before the confidential agent he propofed to depute could fet out for Poonah.

Had this obvious, this direct line of policy been purfued, there is the greateft reafon to believe, that even lefs ample conceffions than thofe which have fince been offered through Scindia, and fimilar arguments perfonally urged to the minifter, would have proved fuccefsful, and that the united force of the Peifhwa and the Englifh would long ere this have acted offenfively againft Hyder Ally, or, at leaft, that by a concerted neutrality on the part of the former, we fhould ourfelves have been at liberty to make a powerful attack upon his dominions from the Malabar coaft.

The Mharatta minifter having fignified his ready and chearful acquiefcence to receive a confidential perfon, the General deputed Captain Watherfton * to Poonah, where he arrived the 14th of January, 1782.

I fhall

---

* The deputation of this gentleman to the Mharatta court was peculiarly acceptable to Nana Furnefe the minifter, fince, though not perfonally known, a correfpondence had commenced betwixt them fo early as the year 1779, and through the recommendation

I shall not here enter into a particular description of his negociation, since it ultimately failed in producing a treaty. This failure, however, must not be attributed either to his want of zealous endeavour, or to disinclination on the part of the minister, but to a new system unfortunately adopted in Bengal, which deprived General Goddard of his plenipotentiary powers at the very instant when they promised to prove effectual, and placed a confidence in the supposed influence and good offices of Scindia, which, even admitting the sincerity of his intentions, they could not in good policy deserve.*

mendation of Dewaghur Pundit, Modajee Bosla's Dewan, he had frequently expressed his strong desire, that an interview should take place.

* The following fact clearly points out the impolitic tendency of the various measures adopted for obtaining peace, and particularly the falacious idea of expecting it through the mediation of any other power, in preference to an immediate application to the minister himself, viz. In order to disprove the arguments advanced by Captain Watherston, to prevail upon the Mharatta court to confide in the effects of Mr. Anderson's negociation, and to concur seriously and heartily with him in settling the conditions of a treaty, the minister frankly declared that he could not but entertain the strongest doubts and apprehensions on the present occasion; for, says he, " You produced credentials in " the name of General Goddard, which the government of Ben-" gal have since transferred to Mr. David Anderson, and," added he, with an expressive smile, " Modajee Bosla now writes " me, that an English gentleman has arrived at the court of " Naigpore, with full powers from Mr. Hastings to conclude a " treaty with the Peishwa. How do I know, but that, when I " have finally settled matters with the former, the latter may " produce his credentials, and declare the engagements made by " Mr. Anderson to have been illegal and unauthorised "

Captain Watherston met with the moſt gracious and friendly reception from the miniſter; and although the latter was exceedingly diſappointed, that the expected inſtructions had not yet arrived from Bengal, and acknowledged that he had authoriſed Mahadjee Scindia to receive propoſals from Mr. Haſtings from another channel, he at the ſame time declared his ſincere hopes, that theſe propoſals might be made directly to him through General Goddard; and even afterwards, when in conſequence of the General's letter of the 24th of January from Bombay, communicating Mr. David Anderſon's appointment to conclude a treaty with the Peiſhwa, and the ſuperceſſion of his own negotiatory powers, Captain Watherston ſolicited permiſſion to return to Bombay, the miniſter repeatedly expreſſed his deſire to detain him at Poonah, until the Governor General of Bengal might furniſh him with freſh inſtructions. Indeed, ſo earneſt and preſſing was he on this head, that Captain Watherſton, notwithſtanding the orders he had received to quit the Mharatta court, where his preſence could no longer be uſeful, as he poſſeſſed no powers to treat, and the miniſter might improve it to his own particular views of advantage, ventured to avail himſelf of the caution given at the ſame time of regulating his conduct by an attention to the general wiſh of the Bengal government for peace, and to the particular ſucceſs of Mr. Anderſon's negociation, and conſented to remain at the Mharatta court twenty-five days longer, at the expiration of which period, the miniſter promiſed to agree to his departure, ſhould he require it.

This reluctance and unwillingneſs of the Poonah adminiſtration to part with Captain Watherſton, viſibly proceeded from the diſappointment given to the hopes
which

which his arrival had excited in the mind of the minister, of himself negociating and concluding any treaty of peace or alliance with the English, instead of employing and trusting to the agency of another; a measure to which he had already shewn himself particularly averse in the case of Modajee Bosla, and which it was reasonable to believe, he would, from motives of jealousy and suspicion, view in a light still more obnoxious with regard to Scindia, who, though an immediate subject of the Peishwa, and one of the most firm supporters of the minister, was known to be exceedingly ambitious and enterprising, and famed even among the Mharattas themselves for craft and dissimulation.

The measure itself may also be considered as a great political error, and an irremediable misfortune with respect to our own interests; for exclusive of the minister's entertaining the sentiments above mentioned, an immediate communication with himself would certainly have proved most beneficial, by obtaining an early and decided knowledge of his real intentions, and preventing the effects of those artful subterfuges, and that system of procrastination, which he has since found means to practise with such success.

Indeed Mr. Hastings himself was so sensible of the superior political convenience attending this direct intercourse with the minister, that in reply to Captain Watherston's letter of the 15th of January, communicating his arrival and friendly reception at the Mharatta court, although a partiality to the mode of negociation he had recently adopted, or some other equally powerful consideration, would not suffer him to invest that gentleman with any authority to treat upon particular points, or even to impart to him the nature of the treaty proposed to be concluded through Scindia, " he,
" however,

"however, directed him to continue at Poonah, to
"employ his moſt ſkilful management and addreſs to
"prevent any prejudice being had to the views of the
"Bengal government, from the ſtop thus put to his
"farther negociation; and finally to make ſuch com-
"munications to Mr. Anderſon, as his obſervations of
"the temper, object, and other circumſtances of the
"Poonah government might ſuggeſt, and be uſeful to
"the ſucceſs of the commiſſion with which he was
"charged."

A conſiderable time before the receipt of theſe orders from the Governor General, Captain Watherſton had left the Mharatta capital, and returned to Bombay, where he arrived, after an abſence of two months and a half, the 18th of March, 1782, accompanied by Captain Banks of the Madras eſtabliſhment, and Mr. Shaw, two gentlemen who had languiſhed ſince December 1779, under a long and ſevere captivity at Poonah, and whoſe releaſe Captain Watherſton warmly ſolicited, and had at length the heartfelt ſatisfaction to obtain from the miniſter previous to his departure, without ranſom or any condition whatever, and as a declared teſtimony of perſonal friendſhip and eſteem.*

How-

---

* As the whole of Captain Watherſton's public correſpondence during his reſidence at Poonah, and particularly his addreſs to the Governor General, dated Jan. 23d, 1782, will have been tranſmitted to the honourable the Court of Directors, any partial extracts from his letters muſt be unneceſſary. I ſhall therefore at preſent finiſh the ſubject of his embaſſy, by tranſcribing his own words from the concluding letter of his correſpondence with Mr. Haſtings, dated Poonah, March 9th, 1782, which deſcribes in very juſt and impartial colours the nature and effects of his negociation. " In the ſeveral letters which I have had
"the

However mortifying and unjuſt this ſuperceſſion of the powers delegated to General Goddard, and at the

"the honour to addreſs you from this place, every circumſtance
"has been repreſented in as minute and clear a manner as I poſ-
"ſibly could; and nothing at preſent occurs to me, as before
"omitted, the communication of which is neceſſary to lay open
"the ſentiments and deſigns of this court with the greater cer-
"tainty and preciſion, than what my correſpondence may have
"already effected.

"If I have failed in accompliſhing the important objects of
"my deputation, or in rendering ſuch eſſential ſervice to the
"Company's intereſts, as might have been expected from my
"ſituation, the former muſt be attributed to circumſtances which
"could not be foreſeen or avoided, and the latter I may lament
"as a misfortune, but cannot help entertaining a hope it will
"never be imputed as a fault, being conſcious in my own breaſt
"of having been actuated by the moſt zealous and unprejudiced
"wiſhes for the public good, land of having exerted all my en-
"deavours ſtrenuouſly and ſolely to that end; and although the
"ſanguine expectations formed by General Goddard, when he
"deputed me to Poonah, of fulfilling your deſire of an alliance
"with the Mharatta ſtate, have been diſappointed, he has ſtill
"the happy conſolation to reflect, that my preſence with the
"miniſter at this time has been productive of ſome benefit to the
"public cauſe, and aſſiſted in laying the foundation of future
"friendſhip, by an early diſcovery of the ſecret deſigns of the
"Mharatta government, and the policy which influences their
"conduct, by rendering the arts of concealment and procraſti-
"nation on their part leſs eaſy to be practiſed hereafter, by eſta-
"bliſhing a more free and unreſerved communication of ſenti-
"ment on both ſides, and by removing every doubt and ſuſpi-
"cion from the mind of the miniſter, relative to your intentions
"in deputing Mr. Anderſon, of whoſe excluſive and ſuperiour
"powers to treat, he has at laſt declared himſelf to be perfectly
"ſatisfied."

very

very inſtant of his commencing a negociation, muſt have reaſonably appeared to him, it is evident from his inſtructions to Captain Watherſton, and from the whole of his ſubſequent conduct, that he did not allow his own private feelings on this occaſion to operate to the prejudice of the public intereſt, or relax in the ſmalleſt degree in his zealous and unwearied endeavours to forward the future views of the Bengal government, to whom, in his addreſs of the 16th of February, acknowledging the receipt of the Governor General's letter, which had revoked his plenipotentiary appointment, he expreſſed himſelf in the moſt temperate though ſpirited terms; and in the language of unbiaſſed truth and candid ſenſibility, while he declared his fixed determination of ſtrenuouſly and invariably exerting himſelf to promote the ſucceſsful accompliſhment of Mr. Anderſon's treaty, he only added a ſincere and fervent hope, " that the meaſures then adopted, and the
" change which had taken place in the channel of ne-
" gociation, might not prove in the moſt diſtant de-
" gree of proportion ſo prejudicial to the Company's
" intereſts, as he was compelled to feel and declare
" them injurious to himſelf."*

Imme-

* It is worthy of remark, that though the Governor General and Council, in their letter to General Goddard of the 24th of Dec. 1781, uſe the following words, " The Governor General " will explain to you, that the appointment of Mr. Anderſon, " as miniſter to Poonah, was a meaſure of local neceſſity, and " not dictated by any diſapprobation of your conduct in the ple- " nipotentiary character with which you were inveſted," Mr. Haſtings contented himſelf with an explanation far leſs ſatisfactory than ſuch a liberal declaration on the part of the Bengal government gave reaſon to expect, and reſtricted it to a ſimple
and

Immediately after Captain Watherston's return from Poonah, and the confequent ceffation of hoftilities with the Mharattas, which, though not formally agreed to, had then actually taken place, by a confent mutually implied, though not declared, the government of Bombay, in concert with General Goddard, meditated an attack upon Hyder's dominions from the coaft of Malabar; and however averfe they were to any inferior attempt, which they were fenfible muft only produce an augmentation of expence, and be attended with imminent hazard, without any adequate acquifition in profpect, and without any hope of ferioufly alarming Hyder with fears for the fafety of his kingdom, and thereby compelling him to relinquifh the Carnatic, they planned an expedition againft Magalore, and would certainly have entered upon its execution, had not the latenefs of the feafon, and the very dangerous navigation upon the Malabar coaft, rendered fuch an enterprife utterly impracticable previous to the commencement of the monfoon.

Difappointed in their wifhes of making an immediate diverfion, they were under the neceffity of contenting themfelves for the prefent with paffing a refolution to attack Hyder Ally as foon after the breaking up of the rainy feafon as circumftances would poffibly admit, and they entertained the ftrongeft hopes of receiving fuch effectual fupport and affiftance from the Governor Ge-

and unqualified intimation, " that he had thought proper to in-
" veft Mr. Anderfon with plenipotentiary authority to conclude a
" treaty of peace and alliance with the minifters of the Mha-
" ratta government at Poonah, and that he would firft repair to
" Mahadjee Scindia, who had offered to be a mediator with the
" Mharatta adminiftration, in order to concert with him the
" means moft likely to produce a fafe and honourable peace."

neral and Council during the intervening period, as might enable them to enter his dominions in force, and with preparations correfponding to the important advantages expected from, and only to be obtained by, a powerful and formidable invafion.

For this purpofe a plan of operations was prepared by General Goddard, and delivered into the Select Committee of Bombay the middle of April, 1782, in which he ftated the number and quality of the troops it would be abfolutely neceffary to employ upon a fervice of fuch moment and magnitude, the expence in which its effectual execution would finally involve the Company, and the fum of money immediately requifite to fet fuch an enterprize on foot.

His plan, though directed to fo grand and extenfive an object, was confeffedly calculated upon fuch moderate and limited principles, in the means propofed for its attainment, that nothing but the moft preffing and urgent neceffity of affairs, together with a merited confidence in the known character, experience, and military abilities of the officer by whom it was to be conducted, could have juftified the approbation and concurrence it met with. The Bombay government tranfmitted a copy of it round to Bengal, defcribing at the fame time their own total want of refources, and the dependance they muft neceffarily place upon the Governor General and Council's affiftance for the means of accomplifhing it with effect; nor were they without fome grounds of hope, from the very flattering and favourable accounts they were continually receiving of the progrefs and ftate of Mr. Anderfon's negociation, that the endeavours of that gentleman to conclude a treaty of peace or alliance with the Mharattas, through the mediation of Mahadjee Scindia, might be attended

with

with fuccefs, and that they might enter upon a plan of hoftilities againft Hyder, not only without any apprehenfion of an attack upon their own fettlements from the Mharattas, but even fupported by them as a powerful and ufeful ally.

I have thus conducted my narrative to the commencement of the rainy monfoon of the year 1782; and here I muft neceffarily bring it to a conclufion, being uninformed of fuch material occurrences as may have happened in India, fubfequent to the following month of October, when the monfoon clofed, and the feafon of action commenced.

At that period the ftate of the war on the Coromandel coaft, as far as the land-operations extended, wore an afpect far from unfavourable, and even encouraged fome hopes of a fuccefsful termination, if either our naval efforts fhould fortunately prove equal to drive the French fleet from the Coromandel coaft, which there was great reafon to expect the fuperiority occafioned by the junction of Sir Richard Bickerton's fquadron, that left Bombay about the middle of September, would certainly enable us to effect; or if any adequate diverfion could be made in its favour by a ferious and powerful attack upon Hyder's dominions from the fide of Malabar.

This latter point, however, feemed to depend entirely upon the two following circumftances, viz. " the " refult of Mr. Anderfon's negociation with Mahadjee " Scindia," and " the refolution of the Governor Ge- " neral and Council fubfequent to their receipt of the " plan of military operations propofed by General " Goddard."

Refpecting the former of thefe, although as early as the 17th of May, 1782, a treaty had been fettled and concluded upon terms, the moſt humiliating and derogatory on our part that could poſſibly be exacted by a victorious enemy; and although, beſides the reſtitution of our late conqueſts, we had conſented to relinquiſh whatever had been ceded to us by the Poorunda treaty, as well as to abandon entirely the intereſts and cauſe of Ragonaut Row, the Poonah adminiſtration had ſuffered a period of five months to elapſe without finally approving and ratifying the conditions of the treaty; and it appeared moſt probable, that the miniſter, ſenſible of the little danger he had to apprehend, and of the unprepared ſtate to which we had reduced ourſelves of acting offenſively againſt the Peiſhwa, would avail himſelf of the advantage he derived from the mode of negociation we had adopted, to protract the final adjuſtment of matters with us, until he had completely matured his own political ſchemes, and might find it in every reſpect convenient and perfectly agreeable to himſelf, to take a poſitive and decided part either for or againſt our intereſts.*

---

* I have choſe to avoid entering more fully into the ſubject of this treaty at preſent for the two following reaſons. Firſt, Becauſe the treaty itſelf until ratified does not in reality exiſt; and ſecondly, Becauſe however inconcluſive and inadequate to the ſacrifices we have offered, ſuch articles as relate to Hyder Ally, may appear in their preſent ſtate, they may poſſibly lead to, and form a baſis of future engagements of the moſt important nature, which it was neceſſary ſhould for ſome time remain ſecret, or be the ſubject of a ſeparate argument. The following circumſtance, however, deſerves to be particularly noticed in this peace, that Modajee Boſla, Rajah of Berar, in the preſent treaty is permitted to aſſume his proper political character and ſtation, and is included together with Nizam Ally Chawn and Hyder Ally Chawn, as a friend and ally of the Mharatta ſtate.

Regarding

Regarding the second circumstance above alluded to, viz. " the resolution of the Bengal government upon " considering the plan transmitted from Bombay for " their approbation," the advices received from Calcutta were not only the most unfavourable and discouraging, but totally destroyed every hope of equipping an armament of sufficient force to make any serious or useful attack upon Hyder's dominions from the Malabar coast, since the Governor General and Council declared themselves unable to furnish the smallest assistance; and in consequence of this declaration, the Select Committee of Bombay, so late as the beginning of October 1782, were compelled to acknowledge that their utmost exertions during the approaching season of action could not possibly extend beyond the reduction of Mangalore, or some of Hyder's fortresses upon the sea coast; and even to operations of a nature so circumscribed and so inadequate to the important objects which in policy prompted an invasion, and which alone could justify the sacrifices offered to the Mharattas, in order to be in a condition to undertake it, the means possessed by the government of Bombay seemed exceedingly doubtful and disproportioned.

I shall here close my narrative, nor is it, I hope, necessary to recapitulate the several facts contained in it, to prove the justness and propriety of the following ideas, which are at least founded upon an impartial consideration and candid comparison of them.

In the first place, I conceive it will be apparent to all unprejudiced and unbiassed minds, that the Mharatta war in 1778 originated with the governments of Bengal and Bombay, and was a matter of choice, not of political necessity.

Second, That let the circumstances under which it commenced have been ever so favourable, the total want of confidence and unanimity which marked the subsequent counsels and conduct of the two presidencies, must have assuredly defeated every hope, and destroyed even the possibility of success.

Third, That the failure of the negociation for peace in 1779, and the subsequent renewal of hostilities, was altogether unavoidable, and a measure founded upon principles of self preservation and defence.

Fourth, That the success which afterwards attended our military operations, would in all reasonable expectation have shortly terminated the war to our honour and advantage, had not our own misconduct, and the misfortunes of our arms on the coast of Coromandel, unseasonably interposed and prevented.

Fifth, That in order to make any useful or adequate diversion from the side of Malabar, and draw Hyder Ally out of the Carnatic, no partial or inferior operation could have availed, and that therefore it was necessary to enter his dominions in force sufficient to alarm him with fears for their safety, as well as to contend with the formidable opposition which the troops employed on so important a service must in such case expect to encounter.

Sixth, That the means of doing this must entirely depend upon, and could only be supplied by the Governor General and Council of Bengal.

Seventh, That previous to any enterprize, it was absolutely necessary to conclude a treaty with the Mharattas, or at least to agree to a cessation of hostilities.

Eighth, That the most certain and effectual mode of producing a disposition in the Poonah minister, favourable

able to our views of peace, was by a vigorous and fuccefsful profecution of the war; and

Laftly, That, when after the repeated proofs we had experienced of the inefficacy of every folicitation and overture on our part, the Governor General and Council were ftill determined to adhere to the fame humiliating fyftem, and to facrifice every thing to the attainment of a peace, it would have been more confiftent with a wife and prudent policy, and in all probability have fucceeded better, efpecially as Captain Watherfton's deputation to Poonah had put matters in fo fair and favourable a train, if General Goddard had been authorized to make thofe propofals directly to the minifter himfelf, which were unfortunately tranfmitted to him by Mr. David Anderfon, through Mahadjee Scindia, and which by the arts of procraftination the Mharatta court has already practifed, and the opportunity thereby loft to us of improving the feafon of action to the greateft advantage, his acceding to hereafter can not poffibly render an object of political benefit, or anfwer the ufeful purpofe originally intended, and muft therefore be deemed, on our part, a moft unwarrantable, profitlefs, and deftructive facrifice.

POSTSCRIPT.

THE very important intelligence which has been received from India, since the above sheets were sent to the press, renders it necessary for the author to say a few words in addition. It is, however, superfluous to expatiate, or enter very fully into particulars, since the discerning public will at once perceive the nature and real value of the advantages above alluded to, as well as the cause by which they have been produced.

The ratification and exchange of the Mharatta treaty, and the successful expedition upon the coast of Malabar, are the two points that deservedly attract the present attention of the nation; since the former is an event which has long been eagerly desired and expected, and the latter promises to be followed, by the most favourable consequences, relative to the operations of the war in the Carnatic.

A perfect knowledge of circumstances, and an examination of the means by which these two points were effected, will, however, be sufficient to convince every candid and unprejudiced person, that both these incidents have been consequences of the death of Hyder Ally Chawn, which preceded them; and it is therefore upon an event so providential and seasonable to the British interests in India, as the exit of that extraordinary man from the busy scene of life at this critical juncture,

juncture, that the author feels a sincere and patriotic pleasure in congratulating the public.

He cannot avoid mingling a considerable share of regret with his satisfaction, when he reflects upon the unlucky causes of delay which intervened to prevent the conclusion of a treaty, until the period of successful fortune above mentioned; a period that justified the most sanguine hopes of an honourable termination to our Indian contests, and must in its progress have infallibly procured for us conditions of peace with the Mharatta state, proportioned in some measure to the conquests we had made from it.

The preceding narrative clearly explains what is meant by the causes of delay above referred to; and a perusal of the treaty itself will best point out to the intelligent reader, the motive of the author's regret for the great and unprofitable sacrifices which have been made to obtain it.

The presidency of Bombay, deprived of every political consequence it had acquired during the late successful struggle with the Mharattas, must now sink into an obscurity, from which it will be almost impossible ever again to emerge; and instead of indulging the flattering prospect of an extended commerce or encreased revenue, must be contented to move in a line the most humiliating and circumscribed, possessing no power or resource whatever, receiving no respect or consideration from any of the neighbouring states, and burdening the Company with a heavy and constant expence, without even the most distant hope of relief at any future period, or by any probable turn of fortune whatever.

That this picture is by no means too highly coloured or overcharged, a comparison of the treaty concluded by Colonel Upton in March 1776 with that now made public, will at once difcover.

It is, indeed, but too evident, that had Hyder Ally ftill lived to infult the Carnatic, the ftipulations of the prefent treaty offer no adequate benefit, or profpect of advantage, proportioned to the important facrifices made in it: but when we reflect, that by his death the whole fcene has been reverfed, and a new fet of actors introduced upon the ftage; that a change of interefts and political connections has confequently taken place; and alfo, that the chiefs who reluctantly fubmitted to the father, are with difficulty reftrained within the bounds of obedience to the fon,* how fincerely and how ferioufly is it to be lamented, either that a treaty could not have been concluded with the Mharattas at a time when their alliance might have been of ufe to retrieve our affairs, or that we did not poffefs a fufficient fhare of political wifdom and forefight, to have left ourfelves the freedom of deliberation and choice, whenever a fortunate opportunity might prefent itfelf of expecting and demanding honourable, if not advantageous terms.

I will even venture to go a ftep farther, and I am perfuaded, the impartial part of mankind will not think I hazard too much in affirming, that the conditions to which we have fubmitted are of fo ruinous and difgraceful a nature, that nothing but fome fecret agreement, to

---

* This fpirit of rebellion has already manifefted itfelf in the fortunate defection which put us in poffeffion of the Bidenore country, and promifes to produce effects ftill more important and beneficial, fhould the projected revolution at Seringapatnam, in favour of the dethroned family of Myfore, be attended with fuccefs.

which we are at present strangers, and an equal partition of the whole of Hyder Ally's territories betwixt the English and Mharattas, can possibly justify, or even excuse our acceding to them.

With this remark I shall now dismiss the subject, and defer its farther consideration until recent advices from India shall admit of our properly estimating the loss we at present sustain, and of comparing it with the extent of future benefit, which it may be intended to produce.

That Providence may fortunately continue to interpose, and prevent the misfortunes with which a train of political errors has long threatened to overwhelm the British interests in Hindostan, is surely a wish in which every real lover of his country will warmly and heartily concur; and the author feels himself at the same time inspired with the most lively and confident hope, of seeing the wisdom and power of the legislature soon and effectually exerted to establish a new, liberal, and uniform system of administration in India, to unite the divided and distant presidencies under one sovereign authority and control, and by directing their attentions and endeavours to the same determinate objects of political pursuit, to render our valuable and extensive empire in the east, equally solid, beneficial, and permanent.

THE END

For EU product safety concerns, contact us at Calle de José Abascal, 56–1°, 28003 Madrid, Spain or eugpsr@cambridge.org.

www.ingramcontent.com/pod-product-compliance
Ingram Content Group UK Ltd.
Pitfield, Milton Keynes, MK11 3LW, UK
UKHW040158230326
469255UK00012B/162